reflections on the beauty

and the risk

of embracing who we are

The Art of Being

Compiled and edited by Constance Rhodes
Foreword by Charlie Peacock

SHAW BOOKS

an imprint of WATERBROOK PRESS

The Art of Being

A SHAW BOOK
PUBLISHED BY WATERBROOK PRESS
2375 Telstar Drive, Suite 160
Colorado Springs, Colorado 80920
A division of Random House, Inc.

All Scripture quotations, unless otherwise indicated, are taken from *THE MESSAGE.* Copyright © 1993, 1994, 1995, 1996, 2000, 2001, 2002. Used by permission of NavPress Publishing Group. Scripture quotations marked (ASV) are taken from the *American Standard Version.* Scripture quotations marked (AMP) are taken from the *Amplified® Bible,* Copyright © 1954, 1958, 1962, 1964, 1987 by The Lockman Foundation. All rights reserved. Used by permission (www.Lockman.org). Scripture quotations marked (KJV) are taken from the *King James Version.* Scripture quotations marked (NASB) are taken from the *New American Standard Bible®.* © Copyright The Lockman Foundation 1960, 1962, 1963, 1968, 1971, 1972, 1973, 1975, 1977, 1995. Used by permission (www.Lockman.org). Scripture quotations marked (NIV) are taken from the *Holy Bible, New International Version®.* NIV®. Copyright © 1973, 1978, 1984 by International Bible Society. Used by permission of Zondervan Publishing House. All rights reserved. Scripture quotations marked (NKJV) are taken from the *New King James Version.* Copyright © 1982 by Thomas Nelson, Inc. Used by permission. All rights reserved. Scripture quotations marked (NLT) are taken from the *Holy Bible, New Living Translation,* copyright © 1996. Used by permission of Tyndale House Publishers, Inc., Wheaton, Illinois 60189. All rights reserved.

ISBN 0-87788-042-5

Copyright © 2004 by Constance Rhodes

Library of Congress Cataloging-in-Publication Data
The art of being : reflections on the beauty and the risk of embracing who we are / compiled and edited by Constance Rhodes.—1st ed.
  p. cm.
  ISBN 0-87788-042-5
  1. Christian life. 2. Identity (Psychology)—Religious aspects—Christianity. I. Constance Rhodes.
BV4509.5.A755 2004
248.4—dc22   2004006854

Printed in the United States of America
2004—First Edition

10 9 8 7 6 5 4 3 2 1

Contents

T here's an art to being. Sure enough. And, yes, I know firsthand how "the art of" gets tacked on to all sorts of things in our time. So often it's a device wordsmiths and marketers use to add mystery and beauty to subjects most of us find dull or uninteresting, such as "The Art of Balancing Your Checkbook." Not so with the art of being. This is genuine. The art of being is at the heart of all human vocation. It's the foundation. *Being well* (or *well-being*) is actually something to which you can apply real skill and ability. It is an art you can cultivate. Or you can end up *being unwell* and antiart and, as a result, antihuman, which is dark, dangerous, and always unwise.

The simple secret of the art of being is that you are free to be. People are always talking about wanting *to be something* before they are at peace just *being*. You hear, "I want to be a writer" or "I'm planning on being the best architect on the planet." Fine, but that means you are planning to *do* before you plan to *be*. The question stands: To be or not to be? Life or death?

Movement toward life begins with intentional being—planning to become more human, growing in skill and ability, in the wellness of being. In short, this means being well and not being ill. Or to be really honest, being more well than ill.

I'm not talking about influenza and bronchitis. I'm talking

about getting in step with the movement toward wellness that Jesus initiated when he revealed a new kind of kingdom on earth and a new way of being human. The art of being is about cooperating with the ways of wellness that Jesus set in motion. Those who follow Jesus have put on a new self, a new way of being that's continually "being renewed in knowledge in the image of its Creator" (Colossians 3:10, NIV). Followers don't work at it like men pulling plows in cracked, dry soil. They cooperate with it, like swimming with a river's current. God is doing the work. He's making the art of being in us. Our part of the bargain is to live in agreement and cooperation with this wonderful grace.

This means peace before productivity. There's an art to being anxious for nothing. There's an art to being at peace with God, your neighbor, your world, and yourself. Oh, what a great friend, follower, and citizen you are if you are at peace just being you. Start there, and you can go anywhere. You can be something, someone! The peace of God is the windmill of being, plain and simple. A living being at peace has Spirit-wind blowing at a steady clip all day, all night, everywhere, and in everything.

Out of peace flows contentment. The art of being is about contentment, living in plenty and in want, in busyness and in quiet silence. It is about having the skill and ability—the Spirit-wind—to be a ceaseless spiritual being living in the likeness of the Teacher whenever and wherever. Again, it is grace that fuels the being. We can be and do after the Jesus way because God, according to his promises, gifts us with the strength.

It is a sad thing when we fail to appropriate the grace, even sadder when we long for something other than the uniqueness God gave us. I ran across a strange character recently while I was promoting my book *New Way to Be Human.* She approached the table where I was signing autographs and, after seeing the title of my book, exclaimed, "New way to be human! I don't even want to be human!" Perhaps this is the most basic starting place: You must *want* the destiny that God has gifted you with. You must say yes to your humanness. To be or not be, right? If you say, "I want to be!" you are on your way.

The fifteen artists who contributed to this book have learned that they are on their way. They're not there yet. But you will read in their questions, struggles, and discoveries their movement toward the fullness of being and an honest acceptance of their humanness. In some pieces you will read of childhood, when *being* came easily for many of us, when what we loved to do reflected who we were. In other stories you will read of great loss, when the value of being comes with shock. And you will read of the daily decisions these individuals are trying to make to find their identities first not in what they can "do" for God, but in God's thoughts toward them.

Each day is an opportunity to live in agreement with God's choice to make you self-evident in the world, to change the world by dropping you, His living being, into the middle of the action. There is a beautiful readiness in peace and contentment. By cultivating the art of being, you position yourself as ready for action.

Then if a little (or a lot) of doing is necessary, you get busy being the word and work of God in the world. If wellness travels with you, if the art stays close, you can remain at peace in the middle of a hurricane, just being you.

—CHARLIE PEACOCK, author, musician, and songwriter

Seeking the Art of Being?

Constance Rhodes

Behind every creative venture is a story, and this book is no different. So before I tell you about how this project came to be, I'd like to set the stage by sharing with you a little of my own journey toward seeking "the art of being."

In August 2000 I left my busy marketing job at a large Christian record label in Nashville, Tennessee. While making the rounds to say good-bye to my associates of six years, I realized I must have sounded a little silly when I explained my reason for leaving: "I'm going to stop doing and just 'be' for a while."

My coworkers must have scratched their heads on hearing that one. All I had done during my short time there was chase my way up the ladder. I was so set on becoming VP (of anything) that I slaved away willingly, giving my job top priority in my life. It's not as if I wasn't doing a lot of good; I was helping promote positive-themed music and artists in whom I truly believed. But stripped down to pure motive, I had to admit that my passion for my job had less to do with the ministry aspect of what I was doing and more to do with proving my value through my achievements. In addition, my natural tendency to focus on my appearance as a measure of my worth had been pushed into overdrive as I assumed even more responsibility to "look the part" of a successful career woman in the entertainment industry. So while there were many things I truly loved about my job, my life as a whole was out of balance, and I was going so fast that I was missing the most thrilling part: the journey. It was time for a change.

I had first started thinking about slowing down several years earlier when my husband and I were in London visiting his mother. Holed up in the hotel room with a bad case of the flu, I flipped through the television channels and came upon a documentary about *downshifting*—that is, going from an intense, challenging work environment to one that leaves a little room for life at the end of each day and on weekends. At the time I wasn't even close to attaining my career aspirations, and it was hard to imagine ever making such a bold move. Even so, this concept embedded itself in my brain and left me longing for the time when I, too, could downshift.

Five years later the time had arrived. For several months I had felt a stirring in my soul that continued to grow stronger with each passing day. God was doing some deep heart work on me at the time, leading me on a journey toward freedom from a lifelong obsession with performance, appearance, and achievement. During those months little signs kept popping up—small but significant indications that God was on the move in my life. I received phone calls from friends and family I hadn't heard from in a while—each asking about passions and dreams I had put on the back burner while I climbed the corporate ladder. I had conversations with new friends that inspired me to take a deeper look at my life and purpose. And then there was the day I discovered a journal from my college years. Written in its pages was my vision for starting a ministry to help others break free from disordered eating—a vision I had forgotten about for nearly a decade even as I was fighting my own demons in that area.

Each little sign by itself would not have meant much, but added together, these signs were beginning to paint a picture. On a hot July day in New Orleans during a business trip, the message became clear. I was in my hotel room taking a breather between meetings, when all of a sudden I sensed that it was time for me to leave my job. At first I wrestled with this feeling, wondering what was so significant about that particular moment. Why hadn't I felt "released" to leave sooner? I had been itching for change for quite some time and had even busied myself with interviews at other companies, trying to find my next rung on the ladder to the top. But at that moment in my hotel room, I realized that God had a different plan. The whole point was that I was supposed to leave this job and not jump to the security of another one. It was as if God was whispering to me, "Don't do; just be." For someone wired to produce, this message was tough to grasp, but God's timing was perfect, and I found myself ready to accept the challenge.

The next day I flew back to Nashville. As I waited for my belongings at baggage claim, I realized that I had absolutely no desire to go to the office, so I went home instead. That night I told my husband that I felt it was time to resign. A little surprised at the timing, since some of our financial plans would be affected by my decision, he nevertheless gave me his full support and encouraged me to follow my heart. That weekend I sought the counsel of several friends I've trusted over the years. Our conversations only served to reinforce my decision.

On Monday I did it. My resolve strengthened by caffeine and adrenaline, I bravely walked into my boss's office and informed him that I was leaving. It must have been the high of the moment that got me through the day. As I began to see some surprising ramifications of my decision, I have to admit I was a little scared. But a mysterious peace enveloped my soul. Never before had I felt such freedom. Three weeks later I left the building for the last time. With my cardboard box full of memories in the back of my Honda, I was off on my journey to just "be" for a while.

Not surprisingly, it wasn't long before I found myself feeling guilty for not having "done" anything yet. To help make ends meet, I had picked up some part-time freelance work, but the dramatic downshift from an all-consuming career to a job that required so little of my mind, time, and energy was unnerving. God was also refreshing in me the vision to begin the ministry He'd laid on my heart years earlier, and it was hard not to plow straight ahead to make things happen on that front. But even as I stubbornly scheduled a few meetings in an effort to get things going, in my heart I was trying my best to welcome the lesson God wanted to teach me. It was time to stop focusing on what I could accomplish and instead give Him time to show me who I was.

✹

At the time of this writing, it has been nearly four years since I embarked on this journey. In that time my vision of founding a ministry organization (FINDING*balance*.com) has become a reality, I have given birth to two sons, written a book about eating and weight issues, compiled and edited the book you hold in your hands, and toured the nation to speak about disordered eating and the importance of incorporating balance into our lives. To the casual observer it might seem that I haven't really downshifted at all, but dramatic changes have indeed taken place.

For the first time in nearly ten years of marriage, I have started cooking dinner. This new development has not only given my husband something to smile about but has saved us time and money and added a little more order to our lives. And that's just the beginning…

No longer a slave to someone else's clock, I often pad down to my home office in pajamas and don't even shower before the end of the day. While I used to spend an hour putting on makeup and doing my hair just to go to the gas station or the post office, I now feel comfortable going out and seeing people—even people I know—without spending time in front of the mirror. I'm not saying I feel pretty, but I can do it.

When it comes to business, gone is my obsession with pleasing corporate America. Instead, I'm learning how to balance the ministry I feel called to with the other parts of my calling—being a mom, a wife, a sister, a daughter, a friend. I haven't "arrived" yet, but these days I have much more time to recognize what I'm not good at, which helps me focus on changing those areas.

Finally, I am no longer willing to toe the company line—for anyone. Instead, I'm exercising my right to stand true to what I really believe.

I'm still busy, but my motives are different. Even though our household income is not what it once was, and I don't have a flashy job title to impress others, I'm happier now than I was at the peak I experienced while slaving away to prove my importance.

That's fine for you, you may be thinking, *but there's no way I can quit my job to learn how to just "be."* Which brings us to the point of this project.

In spite of the way my own personal journey is playing out, I am not suggesting that to truly be who God has called us to be, we must all quit our jobs—or even take sabbaticals from the responsibilities of life. Indeed, the very structure that enables us to experience freedom would crumble if we all made such a move.

The truth is, grasping the concept of "being" requires something different for each of us, as you'll see in the following pages. For some, it's about understanding for the first time that God loves us in spite of what we do or don't do. For others, it's about finding the courage to embrace a story that is greater than the one we'd write for ourselves. It's about recognizing the purposeful beauty of our weaknesses and making peace with the fact that we don't have all the answers. And sometimes it's simply about learning to take time to breathe.

This concept has been explored by fifteen thoughtful and insightful communicators, each of whom has embraced the importance of this journey toward being in his or her own life. Many of them have known seasons of great success, and just as many have spent time in the valleys of loss, disappointment, and disillusionment. Whatever their stories, they share a quest that is common to all of us: finding out who we are in the midst of the chaos of life.

It is an honor and a privilege to include in this book the perspectives of so many artists I've admired and worked with over the years. It is our collective desire that you be inspired, challenged, encouraged, and changed through the reading of this book.

In closing, I'd like to offer a brief definition of the so-called art of being. Quite simply, it's learning that we are not defined by what we do, or how we look, or what we have. It's learning how to be comfortable in our own skin and accepting that life isn't about the trophies on the wall or the Mercedes in the garage. It's about discovering who we are, beyond the stuff, and learning how to be content with that person, for this is the key to living fuller, richer lives than we ever imagined.

Until we learn how to *be,* all of our *doing* will be just that. But God has a bigger plan, one He is gently nudging you to seek out. I hope you'll take Him up on the challenge.

> For I know the plans that I have for you…plans for welfare and not for calamity to give you a future and a hope.
>
> —GOD (Jeremiah 29:11, NASB)

Little Snail

Sara Groves

On the second day of Kirby Nathan Groves's life, we had to bring him home from the hospital. I'm not sure what I thought should happen, but I kind of wanted to rent a room there for a while until I got more comfortable with the whole idea of being a parent. Nurses on hand at all times, expert advice right around the corner, visitors with gifts, and mediocre food that required no work on my part...it was hard to leave it all behind.

But the real reason I didn't want to leave was because I felt as if my son were a little snail that we had just pulled out of a shell. He was smooshy and vulnerable, and I knew I was supposed to provide some kind of protection for him from now on. While Troy and my mom took a load of things out to the car, I sat alone in the room with my little soft snail.

I looked out the window at the city below. *Those cars are going way too fast,* I thought. *Is that how fast cars go these days?* In the parking lot a little girl broke free from her mother's hand and ran to the front door of the hospital. Down on the street a group of giant high schoolers hung out—smoking, taking in the last days of summer. On the hill there was a larger-than-life, half-naked woman on a billboard selling soap. The world that had seemed fairly normal just two days ago looked sharp and menacing now.

Troy brought the wheelchair up to my room and delivered us to the car. Kirby looked like a bean in a bathtub, all strapped into his new car seat. His body was still tucked in from all that time in tight quarters, and his sleeves hung over his hands in big folds. We got in the car and we were off.

I couldn't take my eyes off Kirby. My little snail. Had I ever loved anything or anyone as much as I loved him?

Halfway home my mom turned around from the front seat and smiled at me. I can't completely communicate what happened next except to say that I had an epiphany. In that moment looking at my mom, I understood something. It was as if I had been looking at the world in two demensions, seeing a red world and a blue world, and now for the first time in my life, these worlds came together in one three-dimensional picture, just as if I had put on a pair of 3-D glasses.

I am my mom's firstborn. She brought me home like this once. I was her little snail and she loved me. But I hadn't done anything yet. Before I did anything, my mom loved me with an unbelievable, unmovable, fierce love. I don't know why this thought was so profound, but it was then, and it still is now. I am successful, I am a kind person, and I am an okay dresser, but these aren't the reasons for my mom's love. She loves me deeply because I was born to her, and I had nothing to do with that.

All of my new-mom anxiety melted into one thought: *This is my job—to love you unconditionally. I won't always be able to make choices for you, and I cannot protect you from everything, but I can love you.* An even greater burden was lifted with my second thought: *This is how I am loved—and have been loved all along.*

As a typical firstborn striver-pleaser, I can't explain what this meant to me. I sat in the backseat of the car, overwhelmed. I got it.

God, when He was searching for language to communicate to us how much He loves us, chose to call us children and to call Himself our Father. Of all the metaphors and symbols in the world that God could have chosen to communicate His love for me, He said, "The closest thing to the way I feel about you is what you are feeling for that little snail right now."

This little snail will grow up to make many choices. He will break my heart and make me proud, but none of that will add to or detract from the love I have for him. I will always love him no matter what he does. It's not his *doing* I love; it is his *being*.

FREE TO BE

In his book *Love Beyond Reason*, John Ortberg talks about a time in his life when he was exhausted from trying to attain certain achievements and "trivial pursuits." He went on a retreat in a forest preserve to regain his focus: "I was in the kind of natural setting where it is hard to remain discontent for long. The chestnut trees and oaks and maples and sycamores were on fire with autumn colors in brilliant October sunshine. And something happened. I began to get free. I was somehow given the gift of sensing that God loved me."[1]

The next time he felt as if he was getting caught up in doing the right things to impress others, he remembered the feeling he had at the preserve. "This awareness that God gave me is hard to describe: there was a kind of lightness of being in my soul in that moment."[2]

When you know how much you are loved, you are free to "be." When my husband, Troy, and I are in sync and I know how much he loves me, I am free from worrying about body image and those wrinkles that have been creeping onto my face these last few years. A child who knows his mom and dad love him is more confident to try new things. I am convinced that this is our most attractive feature—not our physical bodies, but knowing that we are loved, and the confidence this brings.

But we can all testify that human love is flawed. In a marriage, love and loving words are often held back as payment in return for the "right" behaviors. Even that intense mother-child bond is tested and sometimes broken. Many of us are so absorbed in ourselves that we don't even know how to love, let alone love unconditionally. You don't have to be alive for long to understand that there are conditions on everything—especially love.

In the most imperfect way, we spend our lives looking for the assurance that we are loved.

Lookin' for Love

One Sunday my pastor told a story about something that had happened earlier that week. He had met with a friend who is a businessman in the community. During lunch Pastor Strandquist was sharing some different challenges he was facing. In the course of the conversation, his friend asked, "Have you asked God lately how much He loves you?"

Pastor Strandquist thought, *I'm a pastor; of course I know how much God loves me.*

The friend pushed him again, "Ask Him how much He loves you."

The pastor said that he would.

"No, now. Ask Him now," the friend insisted.

Pastor Strandquist sighed and said, "God, how much do You love me?" He and his friend sat in silence. There in the middle of that restaurant, Pastor Strandquist was overwhelmed with the answer.

That Sunday he challenged us to do the same. "Don't wait until you get home, ask Him now," he said. The whole congregation was silent.

I sat quietly, overwhelmed. I thought I knew too, but I had no idea—I have no idea most of the time.

The only One who can truly claim to love us unconditionally is God—and He makes that claim. He says that when we were on our worst possible behavior, He loved us. He does not say He loves us because we are successful, because we are good people, or because we are okay dressers. It is not our *doing* He loves; it is our *being*.

I know I cannot earn God's love, but I still watch the scales: sins—1,134,802; good things—1,343,229. Whew! I know I am saved by grace, but I keep track just in case. I know my mom and dad love me, but I better earn their love just in case. I know the opinions of my peers won't get me to heaven, but I better look good just in case. I better do as much as I can to be well liked and accepted just in case that means something. I better do and do and do…

I've been lookin' for love in all the wrong places, and all along I have been loved. I am God's little snail. Any "doing" should come out of a heart that firmly knows that fact, a heart that first is free to "be" before doing anything.

Just as the Father has loved Me, I have also loved you; abide in My love.

—JESUS (John 15:9, NASB)

Being Fierce, Being Gutsy,

Being Wild

Gabriel Wilson

Sometimes happy endings start with happy beginnings, and sometimes happy endings come out of very troubled beginnings. My story falls into the last group. Tough times have often been the mirror God has used to show me who I am in Him. They have also served to remind me of the importance of refusing to compromise and of the joy to be found when I stay true to who I know God created me to be.

I was born Gabriel Solomon Wilson, a tough name to live up to. My mom believed that like the angel Gabriel in the Bible, I would be a messenger of wisdom to my generation. I have always hoped she was right.

I'm your typical Gen Xer: twenty-nine years old, two years old when my parents divorced, a *Star Wars* fan, freaky hair, nonconventional job...you know the type. As a creative child with a very short attention span, I found school to be incredibly boring. I constantly spaced out and wrote songs, practiced beats, and dreamed of a future I was sure would include music.

Ever since becoming a Christian at the age of four, I seemed to know that God had a mission for my life, and I wasn't afraid to talk about it. I still remember my second-grade teacher in Vicksburg, Mississippi, asking the class what we were all going to be when we grew up. Several kids yelled out typical things such as "fireman," "nurse," "doctor," or "policeman."

Then it was my turn. "I want to be a Christian rock star," I announced. The whole class laughed, but I knew it was the truth. Little did I know this experience was just a foretaste of a life lived at odds with convention.

During my early years my stepfather worked at nuclear power plants and was transferred from job to job all around the country. As a result, between the ages of six and fifteen, I moved twenty-four times. I coped with this constant change by becoming an off-the-chart extrovert. By the time I hit high school, I was a regular Ferris Bueller, making friends with the jocks, cheerleaders, geeks, losers, heshers, skaters, punks, skinheads, blacks, Latinos... I didn't care about labels; I could get along with anyone. But inevitably, within a few months we would move again to another city and another school, and I would find myself having to make a whole new group of friends.

No matter where we ended up, my appearance was always a little left of center. People often described me as different or funky, but to me I just looked like me. Looking back on it now, I suppose my perspective was a bit skewed from moving around so much. Since fashion trends were so inconsistent from region to region, I was more or less oblivious to what was socially acceptable.

For instance, when I lived in California in the late eighties, everyone was into Oakley sunglasses and surfer duds. Then we moved to South Haven, Michigan, and I almost got beat up by a kid who thought my fluorescent green, Body Glove T-shirt was too bright. After a while, I stopped caring about whether or not what I wore would fit in, and I developed my own style based on what made me feel most like me. As time went by I found I cared less and less about what people thought about my appearance. I wanted them to care about my heart. And I wanted them to see Jesus in me.

Unfortunately, that didn't happen very often, especially in churches where I seemed to be the kid in the youth group who was most misunderstood. Because my outside appearance was a little edgy compared to the other kids', it was difficult for a lot of youth pastors and church elders to believe I was saved (much less recognize that I was totally devoted to Jesus). I often felt ostracized for being so different.

I was the kid who wasn't invited to pray during "See You at the Pole." I was the kid who was kicked out of chapel at church camp for being dressed "inappropriately." (I was wearing ripped up jeans.) I was the kid who was picked on by the other church kids, who would tell me, "You say you're a Christian, but you look like a rebel." Their words stung.

In my heart I knew they weren't bad people, but their comments did not seem to convey much grace toward me. Looking back I realize that I probably didn't extend much grace toward them either. I couldn't understand why they had such a hard time accepting me as I was, weird clothes, freaky hair, and all.

Graduating from high school presented even more challenges, this time with members of my family who questioned the validity of my life goals and aspirations. They thought I was crazy for believing that God had called me to be a full-time musician. To them, music was just something to do for fun—like a hobby.

"Grow up," their questions seemed to imply. "A real man needs to get a real job." To be honest, during this period there were days when I considered the benefits of living a more "acceptable," conventional life. But deep inside I knew I had no choice but to stay true to the vision God had given me.

After I married my lovely wife, Blurr (a childhood nickname that stuck), my family thought she would influence me to finally grow up and get a "real" job. They couldn't have been more wrong. Blurr shared my passion for music and for reaching others with the message of the gospel. We were already active in a band we had founded that served as an outreach ministry from our church.

Only a year after our wedding, we quit our temporary jobs and raised money to take our band halfway around the world for a month-long ministry trip in Kenya. Our time there was incredible, and we knew this was what we had been designed for all along.

In Kenya we saw God move in amazing ways. On the surface

there were several potential barriers: It was an entirely different culture, we couldn't speak the language, and we didn't try to tone down our appearance or our music. But in spite of these things, by the end of each show, God had broken through the barriers and people were getting saved. Through this experience we learned an important lesson: If we can just stay true to who God made us to be, He will take care of the rest.

When we returned home we put this to the test. We knew God was calling us to hit the road full time, but we had no idea how it was going to happen. We had no money, no van, and no way of touring, but as we were obedient to God's call, it wasn't long before He started to show up in amazing ways. Anonymous cash donations covered our expenses, groceries were often left on our front porch, and invitations came pouring in for us to play up and down the West Coast, in Canada, and eventually nationwide.

As we kept moving forward, the blessings kept coming, including a brand-new van and a bunch of recording gear that we were given outright, as well as a generous donation of money that allowed us to finish our first record. This record soon caught the ear of an executive at Vertical Music, who signed us to the label within a few short months.

With all that God had done, it was obvious to everyone, even my family, that He had indeed called Blurr and me to full-time ministry. The dream that had been birthed in my heart as a child was coming true. Finally, everything was starting to make sense. As our ministry took off, I realized that all the opposition in my past had perfectly prepared me for what God had always known would be my future.

I don't want this chapter to be all about fashion, freaky hair, and music, or even about how all of that is okay in the kingdom of God (even though it is…). But it's important to understand that at every point of opposition to who we are or to what God has called us to do, we are presented with the options of either conforming and giving in or standing our ground and becoming stronger in who God has made us to be.

Every time I was criticized for dressing weird or for wearing my hair too long, I recognized that I could cut my hair, change my clothes, and be accepted. And every time we had barely enough money to pay our bills, I realized that I could get a job, even though doing so would have meant giving up the time to pursue what God has called me to do. But something in me held out, and it still does anytime I find myself tempted to change who I know God has made me to be—even when I know changing might make life easier.

When we sell out for the sake of acceptance in this world, we've sold ourselves short of who God has made us to be. When someone asks us to compromise any part of who we are, whether for the sake of a hit or acceptance or whatever, to me it's no different than Lucifer bringing Christ up on the hill, showing Him the kingdoms of the world, and saying, "Just bend your knee once, and it's all yours." *Just change your appearance to be a bit more acceptable, and people will like you, and you'll have all the love you need… Just com-*

promise on one song, and you'll have a hit record, make tons of money, and then you can do what God has called you to do...

To me, it's all the same. As artists, as worshipers, and as children of God, we can't assume that we are all destined to be famous or influential. It's easy to get caught up in the whole game of pursuing success without really thinking about what success is. Success certainly isn't achievement or popularity. As best I can tell, success in God's kingdom is loving God, loving one another, and being faithful to what He's called us to do. And so, as a musician I am challenged to consider, *What does it matter if we sell a million records but don't do what God has called us to do?*

For all of us, what does it matter if we conform to be more accepted, yet compromise who God has called us to be? As Solomon so cheerlessly pointed out in Ecclesiastes, it's all just chasing after the wind! Are we looking for acceptance? That's chasing after the wind because we'll never have enough acceptance from others to satisfy our flesh. Are we looking for fame or popularity? Same thing! Chasing after the wind! We will never have enough fame, money, good press, or possessions to satisfy our flesh.

What I'm going to say next may sound idealistic, almost like a formula or some kind of miracle, self-esteem-boosting pill. But it's plain and simple truth: *So much of what we desire can be found in simply loving God.* As we love God with our whole being and give Him our lives, He shines through our beauty, our talents, our gifts. *When that happens, all of who we are acts as a mirror to reflect God's glory back toward Him.*

As our relationship with God grows, we begin to understand His character and know His heart as a friend knows a friend and as a servant knows his master. Then we can be sure that as we're growing, changing, maturing, and walking in our callings, God is fashioning us to be more like Him.

As I'm writing this, I feel like a simpleton. I feel unworthy to even share these thoughts with you. I'm just a guy in a band—and not even a huge band. I am not a philosopher; I'm no theologian. But what I do know is that God has made each of us unique— from Baptists to Lutherans to those in Vineyard, Calvary Chapel, and Punk Rock churches all over the world.

Thin, heavy, short, tall, conservative, wild, inventive, contemplative, boring, intriguing...we're all the same body, the same beautiful bride. So let us come together, church! And let's be who He's made us to be: a coat of many colors, of different shades and shapes. Let's be the church. Let's just be who we are. I'm pretty sure God will take care of the rest.

So love the Lord God with all your passion and prayer and intelligence and energy.

—JESUS (Mark 12:30)

The Reality of Dreams

Ginny Owens

E ver since I can remember, I've been a complicated mix of careful, disciplined pragmatist and idealistic, imaginative daydreamer. Maybe it was because I was born with an artistic personality, prone to dream of and long for what was not. Maybe it was because of the lack of action-packed adventure or hair-raising mystery in my own life. Or maybe it was simply because being who I was wasn't always comfortable. According to my mother, my cautious and practical side developed at a very young age. Mom often says that when my brother and I were roughhousing outside with the neighbor children, she knew she never had to worry that I would get hurt or into trouble. As the only the girl in my family, not to mention the one who was blind, I was always very cautious, rarely taking risks. I would calculate my steps as I climbed to the top of the dogwood tree in our front yard. I'd slow down on my roller skates as I neared the bottom of our steep driveway. And I always rode my bike on the side of the street so I would never get in the way of oncoming traffic.

In addition to being cautious, I also tried to appear very well behaved. I had spent enough time in Sunday school to understand that it was important for me to be on my best behavior, especially when people might be watching. I became a Christian at a young age, and even though I eagerly accepted the idea that Jesus loved me and had forgiven me for my sins, I hadn't yet experienced the power of His unconditional love. Nor did I know anything about His marvelous creativity. For me, loving God meant treating Him with as much reverence and respect as I could muster and trying to be a good girl.

But while a part of me was quite cautious and practical, my heart was full of wild ideas and dreams. As a young girl, I'd sit in class and imagine all the fun things I could be doing if I weren't stuck behind an uncomfortable desk being forced to solve math problems. I'd daydream that I was the coolest girl in the whole school with more friends than I knew what to do with. My favorite fantasy was that I had a trapdoor in my bedroom closet. I would imagine opening it and climbing down a set of stairs to my underground mansion and swimming pool. In my mind's eye, my friends and I would spend our days hanging out in my pool—and no adults were ever invited. Most important, in my daydreams there was never any school or any homework.

At home in the evenings, I'd take frequent breaks from my homework to write out these imaginary adventures in story form.

I'd usually stay up late each night reading about Nancy Drew and about the Ingalls family, imagining what it would be like to be part of their stories. They seemed so nice, their lives so full and exciting! And, of course, their adventures always had happy endings.

Perhaps I lost myself in these stories because my own life never seemed exciting enough. Though my story wasn't a traumatic one, it wasn't always what I had imagined it would be. The creative part of me yearned for thrilling adventures and mysteries, and the practical girl in me wished for a story that wasn't so uncomfortable.

In my own true story, the kids at church and school didn't always want me joining in their games. This was due in part to typical kid behavior (someone always has to be left out), but I knew that my differentness was also partially to blame.

The perceptive realist in me could sense that people were often uncertain about how to handle me since I couldn't see, so I began to expect and even anticipate rejection, whether or not it was actually coming my way. I was also painfully shy, and sometimes the task of trying to make a space for myself in social settings was just too exhausting. So when I was tired of dealing with the world, I wrote, read, and dreamed.

When my mom became aware of my struggle to fit in, she would gently remind me that it was okay to be who I was, that it didn't matter what other people thought of me. "There will be many days in life, Ginny, when Jesus is your only Friend—the only One who understands you," she would say. "We all have to trust in that—even those of us who can see."

I suppose I believed her to some extent, but my relationship with God was still more about politely respecting and pleasing Him than about experiencing His love. Besides, I preferred writing and reading to disciplining myself to memorize Bible verses, listen well to sermons, and actually discover who He was.

During my teenage years, my dreams and reality merged in a more sophisticated manner. I took a long, realistic look at my life and decided that if I wanted to find happiness, it was time to get my act together. So I exchanged my books and creative writing for the challenge of facing life head-on, determined to conquer it.

The biggest task at hand was figuring out a new way to cope with not being able to see. My blindness was an annoying and embarrassing hindrance that seemed to stand between me and the rest of the world. I decided to try my best to downplay it and prove that I was just as competent and as capable of succeeding as anyone else. I began using my sense of humor to put others at ease and make my disability seem like less of an issue. I worked hard at making good grades, and I overloaded my life with every possible extracurricular activity. I bent over backward to befriend all the kids at school—especially the cool kids—and I learned how to pay special attention to my physical appearance.

I concluded that if I could just try hard enough, I might actually become that popular girl from my childhood dreams. All I had to do was be smart, pretty, funny, and willing and eager to please. Then everyone would accept me as I was, and I could finally be content. (Obviously, my ability to dream outlandish, unrealistic dreams was still very much alive.)

I would occasionally remember the words of wisdom my mom had shared about Jesus being my only constant Friend, but I determined that she couldn't have been completely right. For me, God had become the One I prayed to for help in achieving my goals and for finding success in this cold, cruel world. During especially difficult seasons, I prayed to Him often and would faithfully trust Him until the storm was over. But when no monstrous storm was raging, I didn't seek God very often. Instead, I looked to my friendships and romantic relationships for the acceptance and approval I longed for. Looking back I suppose I was still trying to exchange my own story for a more romantic, dramatic one. But God wasn't through tugging at my heart.

At the end of my senior year of high school, I caught a tiny glimpse of the adventure God had in store for me when I received a full scholarship to a university seven hours away from home. Finally, something different—something mysterious—was happening that I hadn't carefully planned out or dreamed of. I was both terrified and excited at the prospect of this new adventure. Soon after settling in at the university, however, I found my old familiar struggles for acceptance coming back.

At first I thought to myself, *I can be very independent here, so I'll be just fine, even if I don't make friends.* But it wasn't long before I again felt the need to be superwoman in hopes that people would respect and appreciate me. It didn't help that the school I was attending was well known for its music program, and everyone around me seemed to be consumed with achieving stardom. For the most part I held fast to the idea that such notions were impractical and downright silly, though occasionally I would waver, and my crazy imagination would once again take hold of me.

In those moments of weakness, I'd audition for every music group and variety show on campus, only to discover time and again that I didn't make the cut. These perceived failures reinforced my determination to be cautious and practical, prompting me to major in music education. I decided that teaching music to high-school students was a realistic and personally satisfying goal—I could be the choral conductor who occasionally sang at church. I suppose that I prayed about this decision a time or two, but I was still not aware of how much God wanted to be a part of my story.

After graduating from college I clung tightly to my safe dreams and, armed with good grades and a nice list of honors, fearlessly pursued a job teaching music. I was determined to keep searching, even after the first couple of interviews with administrators who weren't the least bit interested in hiring a blind girl to teach music.

"It's okay," I said to myself and others. "God has a bigger plan."

By the end of the summer, when my part-time jobs were coming to an end, I still had no teaching job. With growing concern I began to question the words I had so flippantly spoken to myself and to my friends just months earlier, and I began to ask myself,

If God is here, where exactly is He? Is this some kind of mean joke? Did I major in the wrong subject, and now He's punishing me? What exactly are His plans, if He actually has any for my life?

In that moment, completely out of dreams and ideas for how to calculate and plan my life, I had no choice but to fall on my knees and beg for answers. For some reason I knew that this time I wasn't praying to get through a storm or to push my agenda. This time I was praying to be changed.

As I wrestled with Scripture, cried down on my knees, and sought the counsel of others, I learned for the first time what it means to be disciplined and diligent in pursuing my relationship with God. As I fervently sought answers to my questions, some of the mysteries I had never been able to solve about myself or about the role God wanted to play in my life began to become clear.

I started to understand that He had been waiting all along for me to come to Him with everything. He wanted to know my questions. He wanted to help me face reality—but on His terms instead of mine. He had written my story. He knew that I would face frustrations as I grew up. He even knew that I wouldn't be able to see—in fact, He allowed it to be that way. He also knew what the future would hold for me.

As I slowly grasped the concept of embracing my story, God began to reveal to me more of His plans for my life—and His wild sense of adventure! He allowed doors to open, and before I knew what was happening, I had the most unrealistic and fantastic job—a job far more amazing than anything I could ever have imagined. I was actually writing songs and singing for a living. As things fell into place, I felt as if God was saying, "Hold on, girl! Life with me is all about taking risks and having adventures. This is going to be a wild ride, and you'll only survive if you look to me for everything."

This is how I must look at life. I will never survive by imagining my story to be better than it is, because God will always imagine it better than I can. I won't enjoy life by plotting and planning and trying to calculate each moment. I have to come to Him, seek to understand how He defines me, and hold on to Him for dear life.

For me, holding on means facing and embracing my true story, working it out on my knees, going to the Bible for deeper understanding, and developing meaningful relationships with people who will challenge me. I am discovering that knowledge alone won't change my view of myself or the way I live my life. And I'm realizing that becoming comfortable in my own skin is not only an art but a discipline.

In order to redefine my life with the standards by which God defines me, I now know that I must create space each day to meditate upon who He says I am. And if I'm ever going to be able to successfully embrace my story, I will have to stay still long enough to face the things I least like about myself as well as the fears I have of being known by the world.

This, I am learning, will be a lifelong process. Some days I'll be better at it than others; I'm sure I'll fall often. But that's okay.

No matter how you've dealt with your story, I encourage you to remember that God has written it, and your story is part of His bigger story. The more we can discipline ourselves to live in reality before Him, the more of His story we'll discover—and the more we'll be able to imagine with Him the story He is telling with our lives.

It's in Christ that we find out who we are and what we are living for.

—THE APOSTLE PAUL (Ephesians 1:11)

Being Present in the Gray

Paul Meany

Niki Crosby

For three years I had the privilege of traveling the world in a band called Earthsuit. In the summer of 2000, we released our debut record and suddenly found ourselves thrown into the much-anticipated life of making music full time.

Because our album was stylistically diverse, everyone seemed to have a different opinion about who we were and why we made music the way we did. From some critics we heard, "Earthsuit is such a good band because they know who they are. They refuse to sell out commercially and are just making good music."

But others had the opposite opinion, declaring, "Earthsuit is a band with an identity crisis. They can't figure out who they want to be, so they've thrown in a little bit of everything and created a disjointed album."

I think the truth existed somewhere between those two statements.

When we wrote our songs, we were just trying to make the best music we knew how to make. We didn't worry about radio success or demographics or how people would perceive us. I think we knew our approach was a gamble, but all we focused on at the time was maintaining the integrity of the music we were making. Unfortunately, while some people loved our diverse style, most people were much more comfortable with music (and people) they could easily categorize.

Consequently, within the machine of the music industry, our gray tendencies made us a difficult band to sell, and, ultimately, we were dropped. As I've thought about this over the last few years, I've decided that we, as humans, often want the definitive answer to the deepest questions of our own existence, and we want everyone around us to fit into categories we can easily understand. We want answers to be either black or white. But I've discovered that, in most cases, the explanation of who we are is neither black nor white. It's somewhere in the middle—in the gray area.

For instance, I was raised in the church and have been part of several different denominations over the years. In my experience I have found that it is not unusual for two different ministers to preach from the same passage of Scripture and make polar-opposite points. How can this be? Could it be that the Bible is not always black-and-white when it comes to explaining what believers are to do? Could it be that maybe that's okay? Could it be that the expectation for the Bible to be black-and-white in defining us is the very reason for so much division in the church?

Now it's important that I set a foundation here so I am not misunderstood. As I journey through a world that I refer to as gray, I do have to hold to one truth as black-and-white: Jesus is the Way, the Truth, and the Life, and no one can reach the One True God apart from Him (see John 14:6). This much is clear. With so firm a foundation of knowing who Christ is, I am then free to explore the not-so-easy questions of who I am.

I have come to realize that my own identity is not black-and-white; I am not easy to categorize. And if I choose to ignore the gray areas of life, I choose to ignore reality and, more important, the truth of who I am.

Of course, many people would say, "Stand for something or you'll fall for anything." Even the Bible says, "No man can serve two masters" (Matthew 6:24, ASV). But while God may hate a lukewarm heart, I've found Him to be very present in the grayness of my existence.

If you find yourself turned off by the notion that the truth of one's identity and sense of fulfillment can exist in the gray areas of life, let me phrase it in a more familiar way: Truth and fulfillment come from finding balance. Balance is that ever-elusive middle ground between the extremes. But while we may be more familiar with the word *balance,* I am going to use the word *gray* because I think it keeps the heart's digestive system working harder.

You might be thinking, *If being present in the gray is a good thing, how does that line up with the fact that your band failed?* But here is the point: While it is true that our band was not a commercial success because we didn't fit the mold of existing groups, for me it was a great spiritual experience. Our band was unabashedly exploring the creativity God had given us, and even though our music wasn't embraced by the masses, many people needed exactly what we had to give.

So while it was hard to see the band break up, I don't regret the way things happened. Through this experience I learned some important lessons I may not have learned any other way. This is where the issue of identity comes in again. During the Earthsuit years it was easy to define myself as a member of a band. It didn't occur to me that Earthsuit was only for a season, and when it ended, I would have to deal with the ramifications of building my identity on a role I had played for three years. I also saw that the human tendency of wanting control—wanting to have a five-year plan—is what ultimately choked the life out of our band. We wanted black-and-white directions to our destination, forgetting that trusting God demands living in the gray. We have no faith if we have all of the answers, and without faith it is impossible to please God. This realization was quite sobering.

So how do we give control to God? Can we trust that He has a vision for our lives even when everything is unclear? Jesus said that our faith must be childlike. Can we really grasp what that means?

These are the questions I asked myself as I stepped into the post-Earthsuit season, and to be honest, I am not finished asking them.

I am gradually learning, though, about relinquishing control to God and trusting Him to lead me through the gray seasons of life. In this process, I am learning that there is a fine line—a gray area that only my heart can discern—between becoming complacent and letting Him lead me.

There is a big difference between knowing who I am and knowing who I want to become. Saying, "Okay, so I'll just be myself," implies some sort of resignation to the status quo. This phrase can be particularly dangerous when it becomes an excuse to not care about developing into who God wants me to be.

For example, if the very character of who I am causes me to do something that makes my spouse unhappy, I have to look within and decide that if being a good husband is an aspiration of mine, then I must work to make an adjustment. It's usually not easy, because change will go against the natural grain of my identity, but if I cherish my wife's happiness, I must be willing to make the sacrifice. I must be willing to live in the gray between who I am and who I want to become. I have to be willing to take a step out of my black-and-white comfort zone and be courageous enough to push myself into foreign territory.

If I am honest, I know that there will always be something that needs to be addressed in my journey of drawing closer to God. After all, if I really believe His Spirit lives inside me and is transforming my soul into His image, how can I be content with who I am? Shouldn't I continue pursuing who God wants me to be?

Once again, I believe the correct place to live—to be—is in that gray area between who we are and who we need to become. But I have to find the line between not compromising what I like about myself—such as artistic integrity—and focusing on the areas I need and want to improve on, such as the need to control everything.

This line is different for every person. It's not black-and-white. Finding balance requires being present, even being comfortable, in the gray.

> He reveals deep and mysterious things
> and knows what lies hidden in darkness,
> though he himself is surrounded by light.
>
> —THE PROPHET DANIEL (Daniel 2:22, NLT)

The Myth of Clarity

Jill Phillips

I have found through the years that I am the kind of person who craves clarity, who longs for stability and some sense of order in my life. I have never been a fly-by-the-seat-of-my-pants kind of person, and I probably never will be. This pains me sometimes. After all, artists are supposed to be carefree, aren't they?

I must have chosen the wrong profession because I actually like planning and predictability. I also chose to become a mother, a calling in which *planning* and *predictability* become humorous words that have no grounding in reality! Although these characteristics are ingrained in me, I feel that God is teaching me a great deal about being open and ready for change and trusting in His goodness despite my circumstances.

During high school and college, I heard a lot of people talking about God's will for their lives. God's plan was—and still is—a very popular subject in Christian circles. We all love talking and thinking about ourselves! Everyone wants to know what God has in store for them, myself included. "And while You're at it, God, could you please be as specific as possible?"

When I was a freshman in college, my friend Julie summed it up well: "God's will is that He would be glorified." I had never heard such a great summation of what I knew in my heart to be true. Of course God cares about the intricate details of our lives— as He has shown time and time again. But His will is that we would ultimately bring Him glory in our relationships, our jobs, our decisions, our innermost thoughts, the way we spend our money and our time—everything. When we think about it in those terms, it puts a lot of things in perspective and provides a great deal of freedom. We may never get the clear signs from God that we long for, but if we did, would we ever really have to trust Him?

The rector of my church, Thomas McKenzie, once gave an incredible message on "our tower of control." Many of our prayers as Christians are simply about asking the Lord to put our tower of control back into place: *If only this situation could be easier…if only You could give me clarity…then I would be back in control of my life and manage things with ease.* What we are really praying is that we would not have to rely on God; we are hoping that He will just make us comfortable.

Thomas went on to share a story from Brennan Manning's book *Ruthless Trust.* Manning writes about brilliant ethicist John Kavanaugh who spent three months in Calcutta looking for direction regarding how to spend the rest of his life.

On the first morning there he met Mother Teresa. She asked, "And what can I do for you?" Kavanaugh asked her to pray for him.

"What do you want me to pray for?" she asked. He voiced the request that he had borne thousands of miles from the United States: "Pray that I have clarity."

She said firmly, "No, I will not do that." When he asked her why, she said, "Clarity is the last thing you are clinging to and must let go of." When Kavanaugh commented that she always seemed to have the clarity he longed for, she laughed and said, "I have never had clarity; what I have always had is trust. So I will pray that you trust God."[1]

The story hit me deeply because I longed for that kind of trust. And the Lord has a way of giving you what you long for.

Embracing Change

I signed my first record deal right out of college when I was twenty-one. It was extremely overwhelming and exciting, and even a little frightening. I got caught up in all the details, from seeing my songs come to life on a record to spending long hours touring and promoting it.

After a year and a half of the whirlwind and finding myself on the brink of making another record, I saw it all come to an abrupt end. Even though my music career was more than I had ever hoped for, I found myself longing for a change, and I couldn't understand why. For some time I had been suppressing my feelings of anxiety and unhappiness because I couldn't make sense of them. All of the pressure and distractions of the business side of the industry had left me disillusioned, and I had lost some of my desire to write and share music.

I felt I was being ungrateful in feeling restless and doubting my career path, but after praying and pondering numerous options, I asked to be released from my record deal. It was one of the scariest times of my life because, even in my discontent, the label had provided me with some stability and security. But now I was on my own.

At the time, my husband and I were still very young and newly married, and we had just bought our first house. Things were not turning out like any of the scenarios we had imagined. I had never pictured making only one record and being done with it all. Even though I felt I had a healthy view of success and had even initiated the change, it was still a huge shock to my system to no longer be on a label. My identity, as much as I am loathe to admit it, had become intertwined with my career. Who was I now? And what was I supposed to be doing? I spent many months praying and talking it over with my family.

Believe it or not, I now look back on that period of my life with fondness. I learned so much about following where I feel the Spirit is leading, even when it seems reckless or ridiculous. The Lord continued to provide for us in all areas of our lives, and He began to awaken in me a new passion for creating and sharing music. I desperately needed that time off to reevaluate my life and priorities and seek Him in all my decisions.

We began to trust God in a new way for our finances. In our short married life, we had never dealt with losing our jobs, and since my husband traveled with me as a guitarist, we lost both our jobs at the same time. Yet during that time, churches and colleges invited us to share our music, and I was able to explore new creative avenues such as singing demos for other songwriters and teaching voice. I began to appreciate every opportunity, every show, every student, every audience member who shared stories with me, every venue that was generous enough to let me play.

Then I became pregnant with our son and learned the joy (and exhaustion) of being a mother. All the clichés come true when you become a parent! I gained even more perspective about what was important to me, and the small details of life that used to stress me out suddenly didn't seem so important. The Lord used that time to shape me and teach me because I was desperate enough to listen to Him. He rewarded me beyond my wildest dreams for taking one very tiny step of faith regarding my career. He even gave me the strength to take that step. Talk about abundant grace!

After recording an independent CD (a fancy way of saying "I paid for the record myself"), I am now grateful to be with a new record label. It is such a gift to be able to start over and draw from the lessons I learned these past five years. That time of waiting was invaluable to me because it taught me early in my career the danger of putting my faith in anything but the goodness of the Lord.

Now I try to treat each record as if it is my last. I want to take my work seriously, but not myself. I also pray to be open to what the future holds and not to have unrealistic expectations of the way it will look. Have I mastered this? I only wish! But God keeps moving me further up and further in—slowly but steadily.

In the video *Homeless Man* about the life of Rich Mullins, a friend paid Rich one of the most beautiful compliments I have ever heard. He compared Rich to the Holy Spirit: You never knew where he was coming from or where he was going. He was a transient in this world.

That's all well and good for people who are foreign missionaries or don't have families to provide for, I tell myself, because I will look for any excuse to justify my materialism. The truth is, even though I would love to be as free and open and willing as a transient, my pride often leads me to believe that I am different, that I can serve the Lord and also pursue the "security" the world sells.

But the Bible clearly states that my identity is in Christ, not in who I know, what I do for a living, what I accomplish, or what I don't. I can't serve two masters, and the True Master calls me to be willing to leave everything and be open to anything as I follow Him.

Jesus told His disciples, "Do not take along any gold or silver or copper in your belts; take no bag for the journey, or extra tunic, or sandals or a staff; for the worker is worth his keep" (Matthew

10:9-10, NIV). Jesus knows that our tendency is to trust in things, in our towers of control, not in His provision. When we have nothing, it must be so much easier to see that everything is a gift from God.

THE RENEWAL OF FAITH

This past year has been especially difficult for my family. I lost my dad in June, only six months after we realized he had advanced liver disease. My dad was healthy and didn't smoke or drink or do anything that would make him a candidate for such a serious illness. Doctors called it cryptogenic cirrhosis of the liver, which basically means they didn't know the cause. None of us could believe this was happening to our family.

I have never had to face something so unexpected and horrible in my life. The pain of watching someone you love suffer is very deep. I knew the odds were that I would probably lose my parents in my lifetime, but I never imagined that it would be in this way or at this time in my life. My mom and dad were getting ready to retire. My dad was enjoying being a grandfather. My brother was still in college. I was now a part of the greater community of people who have lost a parent, and it felt so foreign.

How do you embrace change when the change is so awful and unimaginable? I don't know all the answers to that question. It is still too early for me to understand what God is teaching me—it can take years and years to come to terms with losing someone you love. The loss still feels raw and new. But looking back on God's faithfulness to me through the years reminds me that these are the very times when He can be our Comforter. Death does not have the final victory, though it may look like it.

In time there will be songs of joy again. God promises "those who sow in tears will reap in joy and singing" (Psalm 126:5, AMP). I have to trust that this is true even when I don't feel it, because I know God's track record is consistent.

We can be more transient in this world when we understand that everything here is passing away. My house, job, even the people I love will one day be gone. This may sound depressing, but it is a fact I need to come to terms with. Dealing with my dad's death has reminded me that this is all just part of the journey we go through in this life. It's a process, and no one is immune. But He gives us grace in our sorrow, and He comforts all those who mourn.

Losing someone I love reminds me that this world is not our resting place. The Lord has prepared a place for us where there will be no more crying, no more death, no more useless striving, no more saying one thing and doing the other. It is heart-wrenching when the things I hold dear in this world leave me, but I want to live my life in such a way that I freely release those things while holding on to the things that are of eternal value.

The Lord is chipping away at my tower of control and constantly reminding me that predictability is a myth. I can't control anything. My attempts to attain clarity, just like John Kavanaugh's, are the obstacles that keep me from taking the plunge and trusting God with my life.

We can't learn to embrace change until we experience change. We can't learn to trust God in all kinds of circumstances without facing all kinds of circumstances. Learning these things never stops being difficult, but with each change, I can look back at my life and remember all the dark days He has brought me through. This cycle repeats itself over and over again in my life, each time making me a tiny bit more open, and a tiny bit more trusting. And I know He isn't done with me yet.

We don't yet see things clearly. We're squinting in a fog, peering through a mist. But it won't be long before the weather clears and the sun shines bright! We'll see it all then, see it all as clearly as God sees us, knowing him directly just as he knows us!

—THE APOSTLE PAUL (1 Corinthians 13:12)

Be the Story

Matthew Odmark

Yes, remember your Creator now while you are young, before the silver cord of life snaps and the golden bowl is broken. Don't wait until the water jar is smashed at the spring and the pulley is broken at the well. For then the dust will return to the earth, and the spirit will return to God who gave it.

—ECCLESIASTES 12:6-7 (NLT)

You must take sides earlier—when you can actually make choices, when you have many paths opening at your feet, before the weight of necessity overwhelms you.

—JACQUES ELLUL, *Reason for Being*

Being is the working out of our unique place in the story that the world is telling. We begin by sizing up our environment and then making certain assumptions about what our environment is telling us. We interpret these environmental clues into a narrative, a story with a beginning and an end, and then see our life in relation to that story. But there can be no being without a Universal "Story." Otherwise any discussion of being falls into the purely subjective, and anything that I could say about it here would be pure fancy.

I believe there is no other story line that tells the truth about our world and who we are better than the gospel. There is no other story that holds together the tensions and paradoxes of this life like the Christian story, and I have found this story to be both challenging and reliable.

I also believe that many of you will be more or less convinced of this. My aim in writing is not to give an account for the reliability of Christianity by means of apologetics. I would be remiss not to point out, though, that there are many story lines out there, and we either choose them or they choose us. We should not be fooled into thinking that they all lead us to the same end.

For instance, these days the very existence of a Universal Story has come into question. Most of our modern assumptions are summed up in the notion that there is no Story, no beginning, no end, no narrative. In fact, some people go so far as to suggest that even the setting is an illusion, a mirage of elements conjured by random and impersonal forces that we can experience only subjectively and, ultimately, alone.

These modern assumptions are in direct conflict with Christianity and other widely accepted traditional story lines. So if we are going to have a meaningful discussion about being, it is imperative that we decide for ourselves what story the world is actually telling. What is the world here for, and how does it really work? Is there even a Story to be found? Can it be known and understood? What is our relationship to it? Do we write it? Are we merely actors in it? What exactly is our place in the Story? The debate is all around us, and we must begin by entering in and taking sides.

FINDING OUR STORY

If "being" is finding our place within the confines of the Big Story, then the "art of being" would be to actually "be" the story. This is the meat of what I want to discuss here, as this touches on a mystery that is at the heart of the Christian experience.

What do I mean by "being the story"? This idea I think is better explained through an illustration. Consider J. R. R. Tolkien's epic trilogy, *The Lord of the Rings*. This story has come alive to a new generation thanks to the beautiful films of Peter Jackson. Many people love to hear the story of Frodo and how he rose from the humblest of beginnings to carry the weight of the "Ring of Power" and the fate of the world.

We may love both hearing and telling the story, but how many of us want to *be* Frodo? There is a fundamental difference between the stories we love and the ones that actually live out of us. This is the art of being: to consciously choose a story that is big enough and beautiful enough that we not only believe it but are also courageous enough to live it.

This is precisely the call of the Christian story line: to not only tell the Story of the Creation, Fall, and Redemption of humankind, but also to be a demonstration of that Story for the watching world. Perhaps one of the more profound examples of this is in the biblical account of the prophet Hosea.

> When the LORD first began speaking to Israel through
> Hosea, he said to him, "Go and marry a prostitute, so some
> of her children will be born to you from other men. This
> will illustrate the way my people have been untrue to me,

openly committing adultery against the LORD by worship-
ing other gods." (1:2, NLT)

I think it is hard to fathom what it would have been like to
be called to do what Hosea did. Imagine one of our well-known
evangelists marrying a prostitute so that he could illustrate for us
in the church not only the way we, like the harlot Gomer, are
guilty of running after so many other lovers, but also the way
God recklessly pursues us at the expense of His own heart and
reputation.

I think many of us (myself included) have a hard time thinking of our lives as part of a Story that is larger than our own. We
tend to think that if we are good enough people (for example, we
believe in God and we belong to His church), He will reward us
with a good life and a good marriage. We forget that God is telling
the watching world a much bigger Story about Himself, and that
to believe in Him is to surrender our lives to that Story.

Don't we more often bargain with God in our hearts, thinking
that if we believe that He is in control of the Big Story, then He
will leave us alone to live our own individual stories? But we need
to take a second look at Hosea.

What Hosea did was scandalous. He married a woman who
was a known whore, someone he knew would squander his love.
She would cheat on him and use even his wedding gifts to gain
the attention of other men. Hosea's own reputation would be de-

stroyed. He would be shamed in the eyes of all who knew him, and when all of this happened, God would instruct Hosea to seek out Gomer and then not shame her or punish her or even kill her as she deserved, but woo her. Woo her back. Love her and draw her back by pursuing her at his expense.

Who loves like this? The answer is *no one!* No one loves like this. It is unthinkable, unimaginable. It is offensive and scandalous. But this is the image God gives to His people as the way He loves us. What is already incredible becomes unbelievable. Who has a god who loves like this? There is no other god who loves like this—no one except the God of the Jews and the Christians.

The real Christian Story will do only one of two things: It will offend you or change you. Christ's Story is an affront to any other religion or god.

LIVING THE BIGGER STORY

Hosea was God's living metaphor for His passionate commitment to His people. Hosea knew the Story God was telling. He was pursuing a people He had created whose hearts had wandered away from Him, a people whom He would woo back and redeem. What made Hosea different was that his life became that Story.

If we are honest, does it not seem that God ruined Hosea's life for His own benefit? Couldn't God have just told Hosea to tell people that this is how He loves? Was it really necessary for Him to cause so much pain and heartache for Hosea? Is that not somehow unkind of God, or self-centered at least? These are the real questions about God, the ones that really matter, because without answers to these questions, we will never understand who God is when hard times come into our lives.

We see in Hosea's life that living the Story, and not just believing it, comes at a high price. It comes with many deaths. For instance, Hosea had to die to the story line that said his life would be easier and better if he just did what God wanted him to do. He had to die to the story line that said if he pleased God, he would also find favor in the eyes of men. Or that pleasing God meant having a happy and virtuous marriage.

The only way Hosea could possibly have obeyed God in his pursuit of Gomer was to die to every story line other than the one God was telling. Those deaths became what set his life radically apart from all those around him—and from many of us even today.

In fact, I wonder how we as modern Christians would respond to a person like Hosea? Would we see the scandal, the injustice, or would we see the mercy and be silenced by his outrageous love? If I am honest, I must admit that I often see the former.

So how do we live the Story? If I am at all qualified to speak to these questions (which in and of itself is debatable), then I had better speak first from my own life.

The Making of Art

I am an artist. That is the role I play in the Story the universe is telling. So I need to be awake not only to the Story at large but also to where I fit into it. I need to be awake to the struggles and the pitfalls of the arts as well as to its possibilities.

The truth is that my life is uniquely seductive. I make art for a living, so I tend to live an insulated and self-centered life. In return for this art, I get paid much more than I deserve and am well known and envied. What's more, my art is described as "Christian," so I am tempted to believe that God is particularly impressed with me because of the way I bring glory to His name and His cause.

In spite of these potential pitfalls, I know that being an artist is also a unique opportunity. The arts are the front lines of cultural conversation. If you want to know what a group of people loves, hates, celebrates, or finds valuable, look at their art. So if my art is to have any real meaning at all, it must tell the truth about the Universal Story.

If my art lies about what concerns the world and who we really are, then at the very least it is bad art or a bad story; at worst it is tragically deceptive. So how then do we tell the truth? This is where I believe our discussion about the art of being comes in. You see, to attempt to express art that is divorced from the Christian perspective is simply to fire a series of guesses on what the world is about, to offer another opinion about how the world might work. But to be a Christian artist is to offer one's life as living proof of a Story worth believing.

In other words, a bad Christian artist only tells the Story of the gospel and the way he thinks the world is, based on what Christianity has told him. A good Christian artist is one who has lived the Christian Story and is no longer trying to convince anyone of its reliability. Instead, he is free to tell his own story, whether literally or metaphorically, knowing that if the gospel is true at all, then it must be true in his life first. Its truth must pour out of him. The Christian artist's story must be *the* Story. Or in the words of T-Bone Burnett, "You can sing about the Light, or you can sing about what you see because of the Light. I prefer the latter."[1]

So if in the process of describing the world in my art, I am not as honest about the reality of struggle, frustration, and failure as I am about hope, salvation, and grace, then I fail to live the gospel and have only cast another opinion about the world. But if my story *is* the gospel Story, then it must tell the truth about the whole of life. Consequently, in telling the whole truth, we are telling the only Story that can truly change us. Like Hosea or Frodo, we are called out of an ordinary way of living and into an extraordinary life. When we run to that story line, it will kill all the other story lines until our individual stories, or our very "being," becomes synonymous with His Story.

So where does this leave us? How do we live this way? In its most basic form, I think that each of us needs at least two things if we are to have a hope of finding a story in which we can "be."

CHOOSING YOUR STORY

First, as I mentioned at the beginning, we need to take sides in the great debate. In order to take sides, we need to see that all other story lines are incomplete, and we need to be sobered by the fact that our only hope for any kind of coherence of being is found in Christ. There is no other story that is as galvanizing as the Christian Story.

But just seeing where other stories fall short is not enough— as if a groom could choose a bride simply by finding all other potential brides wanting. The second thing we need is a story we can love. We need a story that can become, as Jesus described in His parable, the "pearl of great price." We need a story that will free us to sell all stock in other story lines and invest completely in the gospel Story.

The Story must become the thing of utmost beauty and value, capturing all our affections and love. This should humble us all, because if we don't see Jesus as the Story worth living, we need to. This is the Story that God is writing into the world and into people's lives. It is a Story that will be written in both willing and unwilling hearts. This is how Redemption works. It is the mysterious power that God wields to bring all that has happened in human history into coherence. It is that power into which He invites us.

No doubt some will be content just to *know* the Story, others just to *know about* the Story. But to the few who have the courage to *be* the Story, God offers a life that is richly and eternally lived in His presence.

I did all this because of the Message. I didn't just want to talk about it; I wanted to be *in* on it!

—THE APOSTLE PAUL (1 Corinthians 9:23, emphasis added)

It's Not About Me

Tammy Trent

Many days it still hasn't hit me that Trent's not coming home. I can still remember our wedding as if it were yesterday. We were both so young—just twenty-one—though I'm sure we felt very mature at the time.

As teens we shared a special friendship, which soon blossomed into a beautiful romance, and by the time we were finally engaged, there was no question in my mind that I wanted to spend the rest of my life with this incredible man I had come to love so deeply. As I chose wedding invitations and flowers, selected my bridesmaids, and found what I believed to be the most beautiful wedding gown ever created (the beautiful part being that it was free), I eagerly waited for the magical day to arrive. And finally it did.

Early on the morning of August 18, 1990, Trent and I met in a chapel on the church grounds to share a few moments talking and praying together before all the wedding chaos began. In his usual tender way, Trent spoke words that made me feel loved, special, covered, and protected. *Here we go,* I remember thinking, *we're beginning our lives right now.*

I felt like a little girl about to see all her dreams come true. For one thing, Trent was simply the cutest guy I had ever known. He was also very giving. I came from a typical middle-class family in which we had all we needed, but certainly not all we wanted. There weren't too many extras. I mean really, shouldn't every family have a Jet Ski, a dune buggy, four-wheelers, a trampoline, and snowmobiles while living on a private lake surrounded by hundreds of acres of land (smile)? At least Trent's family did.

Trent had a way of going beyond what I could only dream of having or doing, making those dreams a reality for me. He loved looking for new ways to pour fun, love, and special gifts into my life. Trent never made me feel that I wasn't good enough or didn't fit in because I didn't have all that he or the other rich kids had. He was the most humble and unselfish person I have ever known—first class all the way.

Greater than any of these qualities, however, was the fact that Trent was a man of God. Faithful and consistent, he spoke life into my spirit every day, gently guiding me toward the things of God. Is it any wonder I could hardly wait to walk down the aisle and become his wife?

Finally the moment arrived. Waiting at the back of the church, I could see Trent standing expectantly at the other end of the white runner. He was so nervous. With one look at his beautiful smile, my heart skipped a beat. *I'm about to spend the rest of my life with the most amazing person I could ever imagine,* I thought to myself. *He's so cute, he's so incredible, and he loves me! Bring on the Jet Skis and four-wheelers—I'm ready for adventure!*

That day I had no doubt in my mind that I would never have to question Trent's love for me. Never did I fear that things would not work out; I absolutely knew they would. This little girl was about to go on the adventure of her life! Little did I know the adventure would end much too soon.

A Million Questions Without Answers

Eleven years later, September 10, 2001, dawned with the promise of another gorgeous Jamaican day. On our way to a mission trip with a humanitarian relief agency in Kingston, Trent wanted to make a stop at the legendary Blue Lagoon to take a quick dive. He was particularly interested in exploring a hole in the middle of the lagoon that was about 250 feet deep. Before his dive we sat on the side of the dock next to the water and had lunch together. Then Trent suited up. He was free-diving that afternoon without oxygen or tanks—a skill he had studied and loved to do very much.

Trent was an experienced diver who had been diving since he was twelve years old, so I was never afraid of his diving or adventuring in the sea. I sat on the dock while Trent slipped into the water. Halfway between the dock and that hole, Trent turned around, lifted his head out of the water, and waved good-bye to me. I stayed there for some time watching him come up for breath every few minutes. As I soaked in the sun, I thought about how happy I was. After eleven years of marriage, I still felt like that little girl whose adventure had only gotten better with time.

Over the years Trent and I had grown and changed, but somehow we still felt as if we were on the same page with each other. No matter what we went through, there was nothing we couldn't work out. Day by day, year by year, we were sharing life together, always trying to experience God's fullest. And what a journey it had been!

Just a few years after we were married, I had the opportunity to realize a lifelong dream when I released my first CD and began traveling the world as a Christian recording artist. That was when I came up with my stage name, Tammy Trent, taking Trent's first name as my last since I wasn't about to use our *real* last name, Lenderink. I had been called "Lendermilk" and "Lenderdink" too many times, and I sure didn't want to have someone introduce me on stage or on the radio that way. Oh, the embarrassment!

Trent and I had always talked about being in ministry together, and as I became more involved in recording and performing, he soon gave up his job with the family business to tour with me and manage my career. His keen business sense and irresistibly warm personality were invaluable as we spent the next six years building upon the platform God had given us to reach many people with the gospel.

Now, after all these wonderful years together, we were making plans to start a family. A few months earlier on the way home from one of my concerts, the discussion had turned to children. As we talked about the typical pros and cons, I turned to Trent and said, "If we had a baby, at least I would have a part of you if anything were ever to happen to you. And if anything ever happened to me then you would have an extension of me."

Trent looked at me for a moment, then grabbed me by the hand and said, "That's it! We're starting a family now!"

I laughed as I thought, *Here? Right now? NO! We're on a plane!*

When we arrived home from that trip, Trent added maternity care to our insurance plan, and now I was thinking ahead to when we would start trying to get pregnant early the following year. It was all so perfect...

The gentle *slap, slap* of water against the dock slowly brought me back to reality. Suddenly something seemed terribly wrong. As my eyes scanned the smooth waters of the lagoon, I realized that Trent had not come up for air in quite a while. At first I told myself not to worry—after all, Trent had been diving for most of his life and was very skilled in the water. But as time passed, my concern grew stronger. Eventually my worry turned to panic.

I called frantically for help, and soon rescue divers began searching the waters for Trent. As they searched, darkness began to fall not only on the lagoon but also in my heart. My perfect world was crashing down around me, and there was nothing I could do but cry out to God and hope for a miracle.

After three hours the search was called off. There simply wasn't enough light to continue—they would have to resume their search the next morning.

On Tuesday, September 11, divers recovered the body of my husband. While we'll never know exactly what happened, it appeared that Trent had died from multiple contusions to the back of his head. That morning as my world crumbled, terrorists attacked the United States, and flights were canceled across America. While the entire nation reeled in shock and grief over its own tragedy, my mom, sister, and best friend were on grounded planes across the country and couldn't get to me to provide the comfort and support I so desperately needed at that moment.

Miraculously, my father-in-law had managed to get a red-eye out of Los Angeles where he had been on a business trip the night before, and he arrived in Jamaica early that morning. After a three-hour drive, he finally reached me just thirty minutes after I had received the devastating news about Trent.

I remember falling to the floor screaming and crying. All I could say was, "Jesus, what happened? Trent, baby, what happened?

What went wrong? How could this possibly be good for my life? What do I do now? What am I supposed to do?"

All our lives Trent and I had looked to God for guidance, for wisdom, for comfort. So even though my heart was breaking and I couldn't understand how God would allow such a thing to happen, I knew I didn't want to run away from Him. Desperate to cling to the only thing I knew was true, I found myself crying out to Him, *There are a million questions, and I don't understand any of this.* As my body ached with sadness and confusion, I just kept asking God to remind me that He was real.

Most of my life I had been telling other people that Jesus was real and that heaven was real. Now I found myself questioning all of it. I needed to feel something—I needed God to reveal Himself to me.

An Angel in Housekeeping Clothes

The next morning, after a sleepless night, I got up and tried to pull myself together for the day. Weary with grief, my mind rebelled against the reality of Trent's death. I couldn't even get my tongue to say that word out loud. It seemed too...final. The rest of my body seemed to join in silent protest. I couldn't breathe. I couldn't walk. I couldn't even stand.

From time to time I would grab the bathroom railing and try to take a step, only to sit down again. In my desperation, shaking and rocking, I cried out again to God for tangible proof of His presence. *Please,* I prayed, *send me an angel—someone to hold me, to love me. Just one angel.* I missed my mom and wanted the gentleness of her loving touch so badly.

As I walked out of the bathroom, I heard a voice in my father-in-law's room, which adjoined my own. I walked to the open door to see a Jamaican woman standing there in a Hilton housekeeping uniform. Desperate for some sense of order to which I could cling, I asked the woman if she would mind coming in to make the bed.

She looked at me with deep compassion in her eyes and said, "I could hear you crying, and I've been trying to get to you." As tears welled up in my eyes, she added, "Can I just come in and hold you?"

I fell into her arms, and as the woman held me close, she began to pray. It was then that I realized this woman was the angel I had cried out to God to send me. In my darkest hour He was showing Himself to be real. He had answered my prayer—and He wasn't finished yet.

After we spent a moment praying and crying together, the woman began to make my bed, singing praise songs to God as she worked. Against this beautiful backdrop of sound, I walked into the next room, grabbed the Gideon Bible off the nightstand, and prayed a second prayer: *Lord, please give me a scripture. I don't want to have to search for it—please give me something I can take with me every day.*

As I opened God's Word, the first thing that came to me was this amazing verse, "Weeping may last for the night, but a shout of joy comes in the morning" (Psalm 30:5, NASB). At that moment, in spite of the heart-wrenching grief I felt, I found myself overwhelmed by God's grace.

Through an angel in housekeeping clothes and a timely passage of Scripture, it was as if God was saying to me, "I hear your prayers. I know your heart. I'm here for you. You're going to be just fine, Tammy. You're not alone, and we'll get through this together—not somehow, but triumphantly."

FINDING MYSELF IN THE SILENCE

At the time of this writing, it's been about two and a half years since Trent's death, and with each month that passes, I find myself in a different place. Daily I walk the hard road of trying to put my life back together—trying to hear from God, trying to stay close to Him, trying to talk to Him. All my life I thought I knew how to trust Him, but now I know much better.

The truth is, for eleven years of marriage, and another seven before that, Trent was a big part of my feeling secure in who I was. He was my best friend, my soul mate, my manager, my husband, my teacher...and the list goes on. And while there were certainly times when I would go to the Lord with my requests, when I didn't hear from Him quickly enough, I would always run back to Trent and ask him what he thought I should do.

Looking back I can see that in some ways I probably trusted Trent more than God, perhaps because I could actually feel Trent

and audibly hear his voice. When he was no longer there, I imme-
diately felt his absence.

Since Trent's death, it has definitely been a challenge at times
to find myself, to know who I am again. For most of my adult life,
I neatly fit into several categories: wife, sister, daughter, friend,
recording artist... Today much remains the same, but I'm learning
that being who God created me to be is not as simple as fitting into
categories. It doesn't always require that I have myself figured out.
This is a good thing because, to be honest, I don't always know
who I am anymore. Last week I may have thought I had it all
worked out, but this week I'm not so sure.

So I fight to keep Jesus in my life and to draw close enough to
discover who He's created me to be. When I'm distant from Him,
I become afraid because I'm not sure who I'm becoming. But when
I'm close to God, I can rest in knowing that He knows who I am.
And in this place, I know I'm going to be okay.

What Was Wrong with the Other Plan?

As I've walked this difficult road, God has begun to open doors for
me to share my story with millions of people all over the world
through various media opportunities and events, such as Women
of Faith conferences. And while it is truly a testament to God's
grace to see the ever-expanding platform He has given me, it can
be difficult sometimes to hear people tell me, "God's got a big plan
for your life." When they say this, I know they mean well, but I

often find myself thinking, *What was wrong with the other plan? Didn't Trent's life count for something? Why now, with him gone, is my life suddenly going to have some big plan to it?*

Of course, I know that ultimately our lives are all about glorifying Christ, but it's funny how quickly, in the face of tragedy, our earthly minds want to think, *Why is it always about God? Why can't it just be about me right now?* Writing these thoughts down, I realize how awful they must sound, but the truth is that for much of my life, I thought I was here to be Trent's wife, and I was comfortable in that role and in serving God with him.

After Trent's death, I found myself asking God some hard questions. *You've allowed Trent to be taken from me, and now You're giving me this big ministry. But it's not for me; it's for You. Why is it all about You?*

In the midst of my pain, anger, and frustration, God has continued to reveal His love to me on a much deeper level than I had ever experienced before. This revelation first came in the form of a song I wrote just a few months after Trent's death:

Rescue Me

I've been strong to give the world a song, to sing praises to
  my king
I've been there every time, the first one in line when You've
  called
But right now I can't imagine how I could live
I've got nothing more to give

I've been picked now to cope with the same path as Job

Hear my fall

I need You to rescue me from this feeling, I won't breathe
　　again

I need You to rescue me and make my spirit strong within

I could fly high in the sky now I crawl, I can't step at all

I was used at my peak but now it's me that's weak

Fill my cup

I can't believe You're crying for me

Father please stop washing my feet

With your tears and sweet hair

I know that You care

Pick me up

Jesus show me You're here forever

Jesus hold me 'cause I need a Savior.[1]

What impacted me most about the experience of writing this
song is the line "I can't believe You're crying for me."

Back in the hotel room in Jamaica, it was as if I could feel God
kneeling down beside me in the worst time of my life and saying,
"I'm going to take care of you, Tammy. I'll wash your feet. I love
you. Let Me help."

At this amazing display of love, the human side of me wanted
to resist such extravagance, as if to say, "I know You love me. But
don't wash my feet. Don't cry for me." But He was saying, "No, I
cry for you because I know what you're going through. I under-

stand. I was there. I cried too. But you're going to be okay. I will rescue you. Just hang on, Tammy. Your spirit will be new again. And you will breathe again."

SEEKING THE HIGHER PURPOSE

I still don't have all the answers. Sometimes things happen in our lives that just don't seem to make any sense. But today I live with a better understanding of one foundational truth: My life is not about me; it's all about God. He put me on this earth not to fulfill just the things I want and need, but to serve the higher purpose of bringing glory to His name.

But even though it's not all about me, it doesn't mean that God isn't interested in taking care of my needs. Every step of this journey, He has made Himself real to me through His healing touch; His provision; the way He understands my fear, frustration, and unbelief; and the peace I feel in the midst of the storm.

I've come to see that joy truly does come in the morning, no matter how dark the night. For while fulfilling God's purpose for my life has come at an incredibly painful price, when I think of the millions of people I've had the opportunity to influence since Trent's death, I can't deny the joy I feel to know my story is helping to strengthen and inspire others who are walking through valleys in their own lives. Even though I would never have chosen to lose Trent in such a devastating way, there's something to be said about living in the middle of God's will, no matter the cost. And somehow, through God's strength, day by day He is taking my sorrow and turning it into gladness—triumphantly. So on those nights when I still find myself leaving the light on for Trent, I take comfort in knowing I'm right where I belong and I'm being just who I'm supposed to be: one weary yet expectant traveler anticipating the day of Christ's glorious return, when all tears will be wiped dry and I will fall into the arms of the One I love. And on that day, when I see Jesus face to face, with Trent and thousands more around Him, I will shout from deep within, "It was worth it all. I'm finally home. I'm free!"

> To all who mourn...he will give beauty for ashes, joy instead of mourning, praise instead of despair. For the LORD has planted them like strong and graceful oaks for his own glory.
>
> —THE PROPHET ISAIAH (Isaiah 61:3, NLT)

The Ensuing Struggle

Jonathan Foreman

Jeff Bender

Jonathan Foreman

S everal factors have recently brought me into a bitter struggle for my life. This fight has not involved guns or fists or a medical condition; rather, my life is being torn in two by inner chaos. The great civil war within me is tearing my life apart. No one can be trusted, every voice in my head is suspect, every motive is blurred.

I agree with those who deem civil war the hardest war to fight. Brother against brother, father against son. There is no front to attack, no wall to be built, for the enemy is among us.

Consider for a moment the vast regions of the soul: the wastelands, the frontiers, the thriving metropolitan cities that exist within. The rivers and the mountains and the trees—a world within our very spirits! Populated by our thoughts, this landscape bears the scars of our actions: A mountain range nearby rises from the earthquakes of ninth grade; a river whispers of summers gone by; the desert peaks of university years can be seen further off to the south... Every memory becomes a landmark, and not every landmark is worth revisiting.

For some individuals these lands go uncharted. The cities remain well populated; citizens go about their business in relative political stability, and they see no reason to venture beyond the edge of town. The government helps every citizen feel secure, and the population has no reason to revolt. Sure, from time to time a problem arises. Conflicting viewpoints will always find each other, but minor differences are soon resolved, and peace is achieved once again.

A landmark appears on the horizon: maybe a mountain created by the earthquakes of inner turmoil or perhaps a ravine cut into the land by a flood of tears. The terrain usually smooths out a few days later. A statue of the almighty, all-powerful soul is erected in the city to commemorate the event, and the citizens go about their business again.

Perhaps at this point you are beginning to question my sanity. "Certainly, our souls have a landscape of sorts," you say. "Maybe even one that corresponds to various events in our lives. But there is no government of the soul, no internal partisan politics."

Ah, but almost every choice that we make is a split decision. You see, there are infinite choices to make in this life, with reasons to rationalize every choice.

Do I tell him that he gave me too much change?

Do I let her borrow my car even after what she said to me?

What difference does it make if no one is watching?

We find votes on both sides. The majority takes all, and the decision is made.

Jekyll and Hyde had it far too easy. The reality is that many more faces confront me; there are many more voices inside my head. An angel on my right, the devil on my left, and a host of others dressed in fancier garb than these—all proclaiming their virtue, all decrying the wisdom of one another's opinions. Bickering, slandering, fighting, mocking, politicking, and warmongering—the worst of the human animal.

Yes, the characters in my story are more subtle and much more conniving than Jekyll or Hyde. The enemy is among us, and I am he.

Though my battles take their toll on the inside, the war is fought on the outside: real actions, real pain, real damage. The war I fight with my enemy is lived out in word and deed, and those who are closest to me get hit the hardest. The people I love the most are shot down regularly, and the fight rages on inside.

Yes, come closer and you, too, will bear the scars of these battles. I am my own enemy, taking shots at my enemy's friends.

And no victory is in sight. Even if one side or the other could win this war, I will have lost myself in the process. Indeed, surrender is my only choice. But will I surrender to a throne that does not choose sides, to a government that cannot be bribed? Will I surrender to a King who cannot be outwitted? Could I throw the wars of my soul on His shoulders?

Losing myself to find myself... Freedom from my enemy...

Freedom from my own tyranny... Yes! How could this freedom be won in any other fashion?

This victory is so simple, so easy; and yet this surrender will cost me all of my votes. Yes, all of who I am.

The struggle for my life rages on every morning as one question rises with the sun: "Will I take up my death today and follow my servant King?" My mouth is dry; my hands shake. The governments inside me cry out from their broken bones, "Let us live! We are your right, your manhood—your very humanity lies with us!"

And now the choice approaches as I come to the very edge of my soul: Do I have the courage to lose myself, to free myself, to trust in the kingdom of the heavens today?

Good morning, indeed! With fear and trembling I am and will be reborn.

> My heart and kidneys are fighting each other;
> Call a truce to this civil war.
>
> —KING DAVID (Psalm 25:17)

On Being and Dying

Ashley Cleveland

hat can I say about "being"? It is everything and nothing, the full complement of conscious and unconscious, habit, temperament, experience, and pathology. It is how we are—driven largely by our perceptions of who we are. Being is a tricky thing, and I can tell you from fresh experience, it's difficult to write about. It can be so easily trivialized into a pop slogan—bumper-sticker-and-magnet ready. I think of Al Franken's character Stuart Smalley on *Saturday Night Live* anxiously declaring himself "a human being, not a human doing."

For me the difficulty lies in the words "the art" of being, which in my mind implies effort, presentation, and goals. I have to say my best experiences of being have occurred in the moment rather than in the mind and have involved simply showing up rather than requiring forethought.

There is also the issue of deceptiveness. During our last move, I found an old high-school yearbook in which I had drawn an X through my picture. The sight of it brought back a vivid memory of my sitting in front of the camera, attempting to make my eyes look bigger by opening them as wide as I could. The resulting image was of a person who looked extremely startled. I laughed when I saw it, but I had a feeling of sadness as well.

I have spent much of my life trying to reshuffle my DNA into a better presentation of myself, not only physically but emotionally, temperamentally, and spiritually. As Stuart Smalley so eloquently points out, it's difficult to be when you are so busy doing.

The deception is this: I have taken it upon myself to establish my own identity rather than to discover and inhabit the identity God has given me. This is a high-maintenance way to live and does not allow for freedom. Fortunately for me, though, alcoholism and drug addiction intervened. Because of these addictions I have discovered that being has less to do with art and creativity (although these things do come as a result) and more to do with dying—or specifically, dying to self and self-will. This is one of the great, though not particularly appealing, scriptural paradoxes: In dying to self and self-will, I become myself. Bizarre, but true; it is the biblical path to letting your freak flag fly.

My recovery from addiction began with acceptance—I have since found that this is the starting place for most things in life. *Acceptance* is an elusive word. It reminds me of the movie *The Princess Bride*. In this movie the villain Vizzini repeatedly uses the word *inconceivable* in response to having his plans consistently foiled by the hero, Westley. Finally, one of Vizzini's companions,

Inigo Montoya, says to him, "You keep using that word, but I do not think it means what you think it means."

I find it is much the same with *acceptance,* which can be perceived as complacency, resignation, or perhaps even defeat. For me it has been the key to realizing my identity, my gifts, my relationships (particularly with God), my condition, and my sense of place in the world. I experience acceptance as a process rather than an event. As someone who encounters the five stages of dying (denial, anger, bargaining, depression, and acceptance) whenever I am confronted with a full box of ice-cream sandwiches in the freezer, I can tell you that I have come to a place of acceptance in a matter of minutes with some things, while others take several years.

Some things I have to reaccept daily, while others seem beyond my ability to accept—at least today. In my quest for acceptance, I have certainly experienced complacency, resignation, and defeat along the way, but the true result of acceptance is a state of rest. A state of rest is not a state of bliss. My own state of rest includes purpose, peace, sadness, passion, contentment, brokenness, longing, loss, and fulfillment. It is the place where I cease striving to impose my will on everyone and everything around me and I sit still long enough to "be." It is also gone in an instant.

The reality is that I experience acceptance only in tiny tastes. It is something I naturally reject because I keep thinking that life should be better (or at least more accommodating) and that I should be better as well. So I resist. Acceptance forces me to face the truth of my limitations and sinfulness, leaving me with two options: to decrease or to fight. I am by nature a fighter, but if I choose to fight, then I am the one in charge. This is bad; self-reliance has resulted in some disastrous consequences for me—and those around me.

Alcoholics Anonymous has a saying: "My best thinking got me here." Those of us who have crawled up out of the depths of addiction with a wake of ruin trailing behind us understand the truth of that quip. For me, drugs and alcohol were the solution to the disparity between real life and Disney—and a very poor solution at that. I am now very clear about one thing: If I am to live with any sanity, sobriety, compassion, or peace, I cannot operate under my own steam. Let me rephrase that. If I am to live, it must be by dependence on God; otherwise I will, quite simply, drink myself to death.

Dependence and acceptance occur in real time, and in order to experience them I must be present. During my first year of sobriety, I wrecked my car so many times that I received a letter from the State of Tennessee telling me that if I didn't employ better driving skills, they were going to revoke my license. I'd had a slightly better track record when I was drinking, but after I stopped drinking, I eventually realized that I was mentally checking out most of the time I was driving.

I had spent years anesthetizing my emotions with alcohol, and when the numbness wore off, those emotions came flying to the surface like a catfight. This was more than I could bear, so I made a habit of mentally leaving the premises. I found this to be a helpful tool in avoiding the truth about what was happening, not only outside but also on the inside. If I was only partially present, I didn't have to take reality on the chin, and I didn't have to absorb the mean things people said and did. But I was missing the sweetness as well—and I was wrecking my car.

I finally reached a point where I realized that I had nearly stopped looking people in the eye because I was so tucked in to my own little universe. So, much like a turtle, I began poking my head out of my shell and holding it up for increasingly longer periods of time.

In facing my alcoholism I did not realize that I would, in the process, gain a genuine and essential part of my identity or being. I was motivated by my desire for my children to have a mother. My family is something of an alcoholic dynasty, which includes both of my parents and various extended family members. My aunt drank herself to death in her forties, but not before subjecting her family to such horrors as answering the door naked on Halloween and then setting the house on fire. Her children are well into adulthood and are still trying to crawl out from underneath the wreckage of their youth.

I could not endure the thought of subjecting my own children to the certain destruction resulting from my drinking, so I surrendered. I surrendered as a person who believed in God but had no idea who He was, as a person fairly incapable of trust, as a person already deeply wounded by the events of my own childhood and thus devoted to self-protection. It was with great tenderness that

Jesus extended His hand to me, placing tiny drops of willingness on my dry tongue, just enough for a step or two into the mystery of faith. It is a mystery to be lived rather than solved, with Christ as Initiator and Sole Provider. My part is the daily, "Yes, Lord, here I am," but I'll say without hesitation that I am incapable of even that without His gift of willingness—the lure of my own plan is just too strong.

My path to sobriety has not been a straight one. There have been many false starts and one lengthy relapse triggered by the notion that years of therapy and spiritual development had made me eligible for the "pearl of moderation." I have since discovered that the real pearl is the gift of abstinence. This has ushered a reign of freedom into my life that has spread into other areas, and I now consider abstinence an essential spiritual discipline. But I must receive this gift rather than impose it on myself; otherwise it quickly becomes a yoke of legalism.

In my case there was no option for personal discipline; I would not and could not stop drinking. I am now grateful for the compassion and humility that knowledge has afforded me. I think of addiction as the unhealed wound in my life, much the same as the thorn in the flesh the apostle Paul spoke of in 2 Corinthians 12:7. My wound remains unhealed in the sense that the most I am given is a daily reprieve, which is subject to reliance on God. If I were to take just one drink, I would be off and running once again, sicker than ever, and who knows if I would live to find my way back into recovery.

Original sin, in all its manifestations, is a deadly thing. I do not despise my affliction though; it has been the doorway to life and art and truth for me. My being does not bear much resemblance to the lofty dreams I carried throughout my youth. I had envisioned a heroic life of self-reliance and rebellion against convention, inhaling the rarefied air of a rock star. The notion of dependence on anyone—even God—does not fit into that picture, and I was more than a little surprised to find that it would prove to be my liberation.

Today I see that I dreamed too small. And even though I am as prone to seduction as anyone, I do know that this dependence is where the real treasure lies. And I know it was God's supreme grace and kindness that made it impossible for me to prop myself up a little better or keep the outside of my cup a little cleaner—that surely would have killed me.

My grace is enough; it's all you need.
My strength comes into its own in your weakness.

—GOD'S WORDS TO THE APOSTLE PAUL (2 Corinthians 12:9)

Sixty-Five Miles an Hour

Don Chaffer

I am in a van with my hand. We are rolling down the highway at a little more than sixty-five miles an hour to our next show. We've been on tour now for two weeks; we have another two weeks to go. The touring life is a peculiar one, and my wife and I have been living it for the better part of seven years. Seven years... During that time we've discussed it, thought about it, prayed about it, and fought about it. We've evaluated, reevaluated, praised, cursed, cheered, and bemoaned it. And after all that, one question still lingers like the smell of burned food in the air: What on earth are we doing?

We feel drained much of the time. We feel dislocated. We have friends, but we see them too infrequently. Our home is poorly decorated because we never seem to get around to hanging up pictures. Or if we do, we use leftover fluorescent orange thumbtacks to put them on the wall. We say we'll replace them with something a little more subtle, but we never do.

I've thought a lot about how our life compares to other people's lives, and I've come to the conclusion that even though our life's a little weird, it's not all that different. It's just exaggerated, and exaggeration is not so bad. It has taught me lessons I wouldn't have learned otherwise. The extreme routines of road life have stretched my brain and heart so much that I've had to admit evidence about the universe into my own little courtroom. And I don't think I would have considered much of that evidence if I had been living in one place or engaging in normal routines this whole time.

There is a common theme underlying what I'm learning. Over and over I'm reminded that it is crucial that I learn to accept reality: Don't live in the way things ought to be, or could be, or should be—live in the way things are. Of course there is always room for improvement in life, but if all I ever think about is improving myself, I miss out on the peace that comes from leaving things as they are, the peace that comes with enjoying life. And though it's hard to believe, peace can even be found in the haphazard reality of my bench in the van or in the orange thumbtacks on my wall at home.

However, because I grew up as the kind of Christian I was taught to be, like a lot of other Christians I know, I am often obsessed with darker theological ideas like original sin or total depravity or "the lust of the flesh and the lust of the eyes and the boastful pride of life" (1 John 2:16, NASB). As a result, I stumble through life lost in vicious little mental circles, all the while missing the goodness that blooms like wildflowers in the cracks of my sidewalk. I am held captive by my disappointments and short-comings, and consumed by thoughts about the many ways in which "the whole world lieth in the evil one" (1 John 5:19, ASV).

Mind you, there is truth to all this gloom and doom. It brings a sobriety that is crucial both for survival and for a proper reckoning of the need for and cost of help. However, if this darkness becomes my sole focus, then I am not a bearer of the good news of Jesus Christ; rather, I am a harbinger of a dim mood, and the sense of inexorable judgment lingers at the edge of my speech and demeanor.

On the other hand, I believe that if I were to read the gospel more clearly, I would find that these darker threads are merely hues in a larger, more important tapestry of redemption and love. God is telling a good story, but in my sour disapproval of the universe, I too often have found myself more like the older brother in the parable than the grateful, overwhelmed, and humble prodigal son. Thankfully, my weird little life on the road has taught me some lessons that have helped me see more of the lighter hues and be more grateful.

The first lesson has to do with constant social activity, which is one of the most obvious and insidious characteristics of road life. I consider myself a fairly social person, but because of our profession, I have been submerged in nonstop social interaction for much of my marriage, and it has worn me out. I can really lose track of my personhood when I'm around people all the time.

When we are on tour, my wife and I are with people from the

time we wake up until the time we go to sleep. We have a bit of time in our hotel room at night, during which we tend to our marriage, talk over the feelings and thoughts of the day, and work through disagreements, but we are often painfully aware that any time we spend doing so cuts into our rare and much-needed sleep time. Then in the morning, when we both long for a little time alone, we are busy stepping over each other on the way to and from the suitcase and shower. And going for a walk around the hotel parking lot doesn't provide much relief either. I've tried.

For years, because I was certain that there was a definitive way to find solitude, I was determined to address this lack of time alone in a severe fashion. I have since found that there are small holes in any schedule during which one can sneak away, and that seizing those moments is a key to survival. However, after years of trying to balance my need for solitude with the demands of a life of ministry, I've also concluded that one must learn simply to be at home with oneself and with God in the presence of others.

Sinking into the bench in our van is often as private as it gets, and surprisingly it proves to be enough. Through all of this, I have learned that God is not particularly bothered by small holes of time or space. He is like oxygen: He only needs a small hole in order to fill a room with life. And I've learned that in the midst of an otherwise frantic pace, life is full of these little moments, these gaps into which God sneaks His sustenance. The trick is not in planning them but in discovering them. And when you do, it is enough.

The second lesson I have learned comes from a fairly unusual experience. One of the features of our job (playing in a rock band) is that we regularly receive extravagant praise from our audience during the execution of our duties (shows). I have often joked from the stage that it would be quite an interesting life if people in nine-to-five jobs received the same raucous shouts for performing their tasks as we do for performing ours. Imagine beefy yells and clenched fists thrust in the air from the sales staff as the boss writes out the weekly meeting agenda on the whiteboard. Yet it's a common thing for a band to encounter this kind of affirmation night after night.

Furthermore, because of the penetrating nature of music, people often share their deep gratitude for what we do, sometimes in tears. It took me a number of years to realize that even when I felt as though I didn't play or sing terribly well, or that the set list was a bit awkward, or that the connection with the crowd seemed weak, somebody almost always came up to us after the show and said they loved it.

When confronted with this reality, I felt I had two options: (1) to believe the people and not myself and decide that pretty much anything I do is good, or (2) to admit to myself that while their praise felt good, it didn't necessarily tell me as much about myself as I had hoped it would. I opted for option number two because it seemed truer.

There was a strange side effect to choosing this interpretation. I began to recognize that the praise had become a kind of centrifuge.

(Remember that thing from chemistry class? You loaded it with test tubes, hit the On button, and after the test tubes spun around really fast, the denser parts of the liquid in the tubes would separate from the other parts and would be forced toward the bottom.) I found that the more praise I encountered, the more my motives were broken down into their constituent parts.

I began to ask myself some questions: If it doesn't seem to matter whether or not I play well, why do I care about how well I play? If the fans like certain kinds of songs more than others, and I'm inclined toward some of the overlooked ones, which ones should I play? Why do I even play for the fans in the first place? Or, on the contrary, why don't I just play the songs they like?

Then there were heavier questions as well: Why do I do music, really? What does it mean to tell the truth in art? What obligation, spiritually speaking, do I have to these people who come to see us?

All sorts of strange questions came up under the magnifying glass of constant praise. It reminded me of an old folktale I first heard from Romanian pastor and author, Richard Wurmbrand, which I'll paraphrase:

> A young, impetuous king, under the influence of his hot-headed and arrogant advisors, attacked the kingdom of a neighboring older, wiser king. The advisors assured the young king that under his supreme leadership, they could not fail.
>
> However, the attack was handily opposed by the elder

king's superior forces, and after a humiliating battle, the young king was taken as a prisoner of war. He was brought before the older king, who told him that at nightfall he would present his young neighbor with a life-or-death challenge.

The young king sat nervously in his cell until, after the sun dropped below the horizon, he was brought to a long pathway in the midst of a large crowd. On a pedestal before him was a small glass filled to the brim with water. The elder king sat on his throne at the end of the path. He informed the young king that if he could safely carry that glass of water from its pedestal to the throne without spilling a drop, he would live. If not, he would be killed.

After some time, the young king took the glass in hand and began walking. Unbeknownst to him, the elder king had instructed the crowd on his left to shout jeers and insults at him on his walk, while the crowd on his right was to shout praise and encouragement at him. The young king made it safely to the throne.

The elder king leaned down and asked the young king, "When the people on your left began to jeer and mock you, were you discouraged?"

The young king said he wasn't.

"When the people on your right began to praise you, were you encouraged?"

He said he was not, and then he offered, "King, I was

neither encouraged nor discouraged by the voices around me; I was simply consumed with the task at hand. Not all the praise or derision in the world could help or prevent me from safely carrying the water to your throne. My concern was with neither praise nor insult; my concern was with my very life."

"Well, then," said the elder king, leaning back into his throne, "you have a soul. As you have done with the glass of water, so should you do with your soul. Carry it with care, and measure your success in life by how well you carry it, not by the affirmation of those in support of you, nor by the insults of those opposed to you."

Now, I'm no young king, and when I'm trying to decide whether to listen to a CD or read a magazine during another one of our six-hour drives, it's hard to imagine that my life is anything like that story. It's hard to believe the stakes are really that high—but I think they are.

When everything shakes down, when I remove all the people yelling "Rock on!" while I'm tuning my guitar, I am left with the fact that I am one among billions of human souls who have either graced or soiled the earth. All of us have stunning, untold value and, despite our many shortcomings, radiate a kind of glory that comes with being alive.

In *The Weight of Glory*, C. S. Lewis wrote about the need to recognize the glory of being human:

It is a serious thing to live in a society of possible gods and goddesses, to remember that the dullest and most uninteresting person you can talk to may one day be a creature which...you would be strongly tempted to worship, or else a horror and a corruption such as you now meet, if at all, only in a nightmare.... It is in the light of these overwhelming possibilities, it is with the awe and circumspection proper to them, that we should conduct all our dealings with one another, all friendships, all loves, all play, all politics.[1]

Sobering words.

Lewis went on to warn us against becoming too interested in our own glory and pointed out that we would do better to acknowledge the glory of our neighbors more than our own. While I agree with this caution against narcissism, I also feel that in many ways our current culture pulls us to a commonly held sense of smallness and staggering self-hatred. In light of this cultural neurosis, I think we would do well not only to regard one another with increased awe but to treat ourselves with at least the same respect and consideration we feel we owe our fellow human beings. When I do this, both the praise of an adoring crowd and the mundane reality of another six hours in the van fade into the background, and it becomes possible to live from the true center where God abides with me.

Increasingly, I look for words like Lewis's to bring me to that center. Life is not a game, nor is it merely a concert. It is not something I should seek to master for the sake of my own pleasure, or for the praise of those around me. It is a holy, remarkable gift that carries with it both high stakes and tremendous possibilities—and I am eager to live it in as true a way as I know how.

So I think I'm going to listen to a CD now, and I'm going to trust that while my choice and my circumstances may be mundane, I am not in fact mundane, and that, in the midst of my otherwise boring ramble down this stretch of highway, there is a hole big enough for God to slip through and fill my life with the air I so desperately need to breathe.

Let righteousness burst into blossom
    and peace abound until the moon fades to nothing.

—KING SOLOMON (Psalm 72:7)

The Value of Wasting Time

Lori Chaffer

Ben Pearson

I woke up tired today, really tired. Then for three hours I didn't do much of anything and felt guilty about it the whole time. Finally, it dawned on me that I'm feeling sick—sore throaty and headachy. Now I have a slightly better excuse for doing nothing, but the guilt still lingers.

This sense of responsibility to use time well is common in my life. I'm a full-time musician, but I have always grappled with what my life as an artist is supposed to look like. For example, lately I've begun to spend more time reading various books and magazines just to take in stories and information. But while swimming in a river of ideas is good for my creativity, it doesn't bear obvious fruit—and it doesn't pay the bills.

Even now I am nagged by images of my dirty kitchen, piles of laundry, personal finances waiting to be configured for tax day, and a long list of things to do for next month's tour. Aren't these things more important than spending hours reading books? Even for an artist, it's hard to value the immeasurable.

Some say this need to assess our usefulness is a problem with people in Western civilizations. We too quickly divide all of life into the productive and the wasteful. What isn't measurable is useless. Even members of the church have fallen into this behavioral trap. We spend so much of our time presenting evidence to donors that work is being done and "progress" is being made: The 10/40 Window is getting smaller; we've translated the Bible into twenty more languages; 150 people were saved or "touched" this month.

We are paranoid of looking as if we're doing nothing, and even more paranoid of showing our true emotions. (Do any churches sing laments anymore?) Ultimately, however, this is a human problem. We don't know how to deal with the many areas of our lives that defy measurement, that don't bear obvious fruit.

But Jesus is the great I AM. He's not the great I DO or the great I WILL. His life began with an almost total silence that lasted for thirty years. And then when He finally began His public ministry, many people were disappointed that He didn't do bigger, more far-reaching things. They expected Him to become the king of Israel, to set everything right, everywhere. Instead, He healed sporadically and taught about how to live everyday life.

There were no big Jesus-Heals-'Em-All conventions. While He did the occasional large-scale miracle (such as feeding the five thousand and healing all the sick in a village), for the most part, it was a crippled guy here, a bleeding woman there, a demoniac at the edge of town. And then, strangely, Jesus asked many of these people to keep it to themselves, not to let the word get out that He had healed them. His disciples must have wondered why a guy with so much power didn't do more with it.

As for His teaching, in many cases it's hard to tell if what Jesus said stuck and made a real difference in people's lives. Did the rich young ruler give up his riches? Did the prostitute go and sin no more? And of those who were delivered of demons, how many saw the demons come back? We don't know. But I find comfort in the fact that Jesus also suffered the pain of seeing people reject truth and goodness—and reject Him.

Not everything Jesus touched turned to gold. After all, though divine, He chose to be human. He understood that to live is to face disappointment and loss, to waste time on things and people, and to be unable to control others. He submitted Himself to our choices.

I feel less alone when I remember that Christ was also unable to measure the immediate value of how He spent His time. Consequently, I am more able to be okay with those moments when I feel lost. Christ and I are in fellowship through these common sufferings.

Antoine de Saint Exupéry's short novel *The Little Prince* says it profoundly. Before the main character, the prince, parts ways with his friend the fox, the fox tells the prince a secret. It's about the prince's most treasured possession, a rose:

"Goodbye," said the fox. "And now here is my secret, a very simple secret: It is only with the heart that one can see rightly; what is essential is invisible to the eye...."

"It is the time you have wasted for your rose that makes your rose so important...."

"Men have forgotten this truth," said the fox. "But you must not forget it."[1]

In the end it turns out that to live and to love is to waste time. Jesus had only thirty-three years on the earth. We don't know much about what He did during the first thirty years, and for the last three, He appeared to "waste" time wandering around interacting with people. Maybe we would be better off doing more wasteful things in our lives and embracing just being alive. One gets the strong impression that wasting time is one of God's favorite things to do.

Are you tired? Worn out? Burned out on religion?
Come to me.... I'll show you how to take a real rest.

—JESUS (Matthew 11:28)

The Curiosity of God

Linford Detweiler

Jinford Detweiler

I 'm sitting high on a hill above a bend in the Ohio River; the rare January sun is on my face and on the water. I can see Kentucky on the other side, rows of white houses on hills, bare trees, a few hopeful steeples. Two barges pass each other, one sliding upstream, one down. I can hear the persistent hum of the city at work in the distance—cars crossing a suspension bridge, the downshift of a semi, the creak and grind of an iron crane unloading a docked barge.

The nude lines of the trees between the blazing river and me are darker even than my wife's coffee. I imagine some lonesome midnight writer dipping his pen toward the slick branches for a deeper blackness, black enough to praise, black enough to ink the soul out in wet words.

Any moment of deliberate solitude is a hard-won gift these days, and I unwrap this unusually mild winter morning with a mind that seems disbelieving of its freedom to fly anywhere it chooses. My senses can't seem to drink deeply enough the bright play of winter light.

I think to myself after a few minutes, *The muddy river is a trembling skim of silver milk.*

I stare into the rippling dizziness and hear a voice: *Write it down.*

A cardinal whips through the bushes leaving a smear of red in the air.

Am I writing a story with my life? Are my days pages? My years chapters? It feels that way.

I am born into a particular set of circumstances—not of my choosing. I soon become both protagonist and antagonist in my own life story. A plot emerges that is sometimes lost, often revised.

A growing cast of characters takes shape and shifts over time—new breathing, laughing, wounded humans enter my life as others exit.

I befriend, love, and betray.

I teach and am taught.

I come to know remorse.

I begin the work of learning to forgive myself and others.

Some of what happens seems so significant at the time but loses its vividness in later chapters. Other moments, which seemed so insignificant—hardly worth mentioning, grow exponentially in significance as the days grow into years.

I have discovered that it's vital for me to nurture the inner solitude that allows for space and time to reflect on the pages I've helped write so far with my life. The story I'm writing with my life is full of clues. Who am I? What must I do to make my life a true story?

Slowly I learn to accept and even love my life story. I grow less interested in trading my story for someone else's. I want to take care of my own story and encourage others to do the same. I want the ability to read my life, and hopefully understand much of it. I don't want to find out too late that I inadvertently crossed out most of the good parts.

When I was younger, I scribbled plans for chapters filled with excitement, exploration, new love, new places, and the wild unknown. I believed just about anything could happen.

I wanted to discover my own great adventure and drown there.

I wanted bold strokes.

I wanted to pierce the din of the world with my own voice.

Against all odds I wanted to give the world an undeniable gift of some kind. Eventually, as you might have guessed, I had the audacity to begin thinking of myself as an artist. And tangled up in this longing to discover my true place of birth was a ragged prayer I still sometimes toss at the sky. *God,* I pray, *by some miracle, make my life a work of art.*

What does it look and feel like to live artfully?

I think to myself that I could begin the work of answering this question in ways that might actually be of use to someone if I weren't drunk on the sky. I have a problem with these clouds that loom and sleigh across the basking blue floor of heaven: I get lost in that white-as-bone, icy fluff. It sometimes feels as if the sky, maybe more than anything else, will ultimately break my heart.

The stillness of a new morning can make me unspeakably sad. I don't know why. I don't know why tears sometimes come to our eyes when we're handed a gift. Joy and sadness do seem to well from the same place.

If you, like me, have leanings toward seeing these days as gifts—wrapped slabs of infinity, blank pages in a book that we are invited in whispers by life itself to write, pages that later can be truly read only with the heart—then you will be haunted by an array of questions.

Who is the unseen Giver of these days?

How can I leave some token behind with my life, some memento of gratitude for the privilege of having been alive in this blushingly beautiful, yet thorny world?

Why have I seldom gone hungry, while others elsewhere on the earth ache and scrounge for scraps of food?

Why was I not subjected to the withering gunfire of a world war, while young men of different generations held their dying friends as blood soaked the ground?

Although I am haunted by these questions, I gradually learn to make peace with my ineptness, my lostness, my inability to answer many of life's questions neatly, definitively, once and for all. I come to realize, youthful exuberance notwithstanding, that I may well have nothing great or profound to offer this world. Instead, I learn to savor the moments that seem to grace each of us continually. I learn to write these moments as well as I am able in my book of life, and live them deliciously. This is how I say thank you.

I recognize at any moment I could turn the page and read: The End. We're all terminal after all. But in the meanwhile, by God, I hope to pay attention.

My mind thumbs through the pages of recent days. I see myself at a meal with a handful of people I look forward to growing old with. We are blessed with wine-filled glasses for the moment, and the food was prepared with love. We talk together, and the stories we're all writing with our lives spill out and intermingle. We compare notes. The light is warm. A simple meal shared with a few faithful friends—how do I cram the wealth of this onto any one page of my book?

I see myself at the piano at home in the morning when the rest of the house is asleep. Our cat, Oskar, sits with me on the bench up against my right thigh and seems to listen. His ears twitch. J. S. Bach wrote keyboard pieces for his children, and Oskar and I marvel lately at this music's richness, the simultaneous simplicity and complexity.

I see myself speaking to an old man named Edward in the nursing home—he used to be in advertising. He thinks he needs to delegate some unfinished projects to me that linger in the shadowy places of his mind. He picks up a pencil and tries to tuck it behind his ear. His ear is too old and brittle to hold the pencil. He licks his index finger and begins paging slowly through a binder of advertisements that he has torn from magazines lying around. He comments on the type styles. "Clever," he says. But his brain can't keep it together. I listen as well as I can. His voice is weathered like an old love song after a long day's work. "Save a wheelchair for me, Edward. I won't be young forever."

I see myself coming home, and my wife is weeping softly at the piano, her face down in the bend of her arm, her notebook open. I remember reading a few nights earlier in a book by Kathleen Norris called *The Cloister Walk:* "Weeping is an ordinary but valuable part of the writing process." I hold my love for a little while and speak a few words in hopes of comforting her; later we laugh, and she beats me soundly at Scrabble. We are trying to make our first baby. And we do like to lie in bed together on these dark winter evenings and read, each of us lost in the stories of others, occasionally laughing out loud.

I see myself slip out into the night to walk the dog in the snow, flakes falling the size of silver dollars, each street lamp its own unique snow globe. Willow gives her hide a shake, and her dog collar jingles. The night is a black-and-white film.

I see our family at Christmas buying a goat and some chickens for a family less fortunate than ours. The victories are tiny. The moments are fleeting but reek of infinity.

I once believed that if I could get enough people clapping, life would somehow be a thrill. If I could write my name on something big enough, my life would be worthwhile, infused with meaning. I see things differently now.

I still reach at times for a wildness—for something untamed in my life.

I still write songs, and who knows what will come of them. But it's this everyday beauty that interests and captivates me more and more.

What makes for a good story is not necessarily a thrill-a-minute plot, but an eye for detail, loaded moments. It's the so-called mundane that is most often chock-full of the eternal.

I stare at this river in the sun.

I do love days when I get to sneak away alone and get quiet, let the noisy world fade into the background.

I open my book.

I take a deep breath. I can dive in anywhere I please.

I close my eyes, and we are moving.

I can hear God laughing in the background. This is good; this is good.

Maybe God loves these stories we write with our lives. Maybe God is supremely curious to see what will happen next. Maybe God weeps with us.

I open my eyes, lean forward, and begin moving my pen. I cover my work just for fun. But I keep writing.

So how about you? Ever get the feeling that God is reading over your shoulder?

How precious and weighty also are Your thoughts to me, O God! How vast is the sum of them!

—KING DAVID (PSALM 139:17, AMP)

Becoming—The Girl in the Mirror

Christine Dente

Jimmy Abegg

Christine Dente

B ecoming is timeless, yet it requires moving through time. It is existence beyond place, yet headed toward a destination. Becoming is also remembering how we were meant to be... Ah, words. I love them and I hate them. Sometimes they say exactly what I want them to, but at other times they refuse to even speak. On a good day they give just enough to convey an idea while leaving lots of room for wonder. On a bad day they cloud my vision and crowd out my ideas, refusing to take any shape.

Songwriting, like most art, allows the luxury of creating from passion without having to spell it out, so to speak. In pop music you get three and a half minutes to tell your story while leaving lots of room for interpretation—think U2 and other artists who draw us in without supplying too many definitions.

As an artist I try to balance on the fine line of creativity without leaning too far to the right or to the left. On one hand, I want to share my passion and message in a coherent way. On the other, I don't want to destroy the beauty of personal interpretation by leaving nothing to the imagination. When I write a song, I try to paint a picture of words and sounds that draws the heart and mind to visit again and again, looking for new layers of meaning.

But on these pages I want to build a broader bridge, tell my story with a few more words. If these words accurately reflect the paradoxes of growing older to reach an ageless place and of up-heavals that smooth the road to peace, then I'll know I'm getting somewhere.

So back to "becoming." What is it exactly? I'm not sure, but I wrote a song about it and will expand the journey here.

*

As a little child I didn't care about time. I let my mother keep it for me, and she became the measure of my perception of a day. Engaged in the timelessness of play, I lived in increments of the here and now, unaware even of self. But as I got older, I began to see the complications of time. I became aware of change and its effect on me.

> These are my sidewalks
> They wound around the neighborhood
> Always led me straight and safely home
> But now they're uneven

'Cause roots move beneath them
And time won't leave well enough alone[1]

Time is problematic. It just won't let things be. Hit a stride one year, then hit a snag the next. In those early years the ground beneath my feet was shifting. My parents divorced. I was growing up. Moving outside the neighborhood. It was all upheaval. Some of my security and comfort were slipping away. The once-solid sidewalks of early childhood now tripped me up when I didn't watch where I was going.

Back then I was always trying to make my way safely home. As a young child, home was as simple as sidewalks leading me up to a red brick house. Later I was still trying to find home, but it had become more complicated, less solid.

When I was about ten years old, we moved out of our house into a mobile home. Up to that time the mirror had held no interest for me, had no power over me. But then I saw a photograph that changed everything. There we were, my sister and I, in our swimsuits in front of the creek. And there was my stomach, sticking out like a little girl's will. For the first time I felt self-conscious. *Is that really how I look? Time to keep that in check...* I was becoming more aware of people's perceptions. What do I see, what do they see, what do I care?

Not many years later, I led a tour around our middle school for some visiting students. At the end of my presentation, a boy about my age asked me, "Are you a boy or a girl?" No big deal, right? I didn't care that much about how I looked. Ah, but I remember it so vividly. Like those school pictures that became yearly sources of self-evaluation—the various stages of beaver teeth before the backdrop of awkward smiles and not-quite-right hairstyles left lasting impressions on me. Who was I becoming?

> I had been trying to smooth these stones
> Thought I could make my way alone

As a teenager I went looking for home in adolescent ideals. I held up my mirror for the reflection of my peers, letting their opinions influence and define me. I also found a measure of beauty through the sliding scales of television definitions and boyfriend acquisitions. I got good at attracting attention and found myself more comfortable hanging out with the guys. I'd seen my dad's magazines, too, and read those passed-around-under-the-desk books at school. I'd heard the way boys talked and learned about what they wanted. And so grew both my thirst for admiration and my aversion to even needing it in the first place. What's a girl to do?

> I tried the whimsical, gauzy pink dresses
> That spin in the wind when you twirl
> But somehow the princess gown
> Never did fit this girl
> So I fled the garden for the tower

At some point in high school, someone ascribed to me the title "Cold as Ice" from the popular song by rock group Foreigner. I guess I'd earned this branding with my aloof, ivory-tower stance. By that time I had compared my face and heart to the perfection I thought everyone wanted and found them both severely lacking. Determined to maintain the impression I wanted to give, I had begun using makeup, and the mirror was now a fickle friend and a taskmaster. So I had come to discover a certain power in being unknown and unknowable. What would become of me?

I had been hiding behind these stones
Thought I'd be well enough alone

Oh, but I had a better Friend and a stronger Master: Christ. At eighteen I knew Him. College proved a tough test for my new faith, yet He pursued me relentlessly. Many levels of painful growth ensued. Somewhere in the thick of things, my Father sent someone to love me as Christ loved. Scott had the arms of acceptance and the eyes of adoration I ached for.

Then you came nearer
You held the mirror
I saw myself there in your eyes

In this new relationship, I began to sense the kind of love and acceptance that Jesus says He has for me. (I am His beloved and

His desire is for me.) Now after sixteen years of marriage, my husband still calls me beautiful and reflects the love of Jesus for me every day.

> And I had been running
> Still you pursued
> I watched you move each heavy stone
> The thorns around me tore your skin
> But you kept coming through
> 'Cause you won't leave well enough alone

Today I'm still making my way home as God continues to smooth and move some of the heavy stones in my heart. The timing couldn't be better. As I get older I sense I must trust less in what I see when I brush past the bathroom mirror and turn more to what I hear from my Father, who has loved me from the foundation of the world.

> I am becoming what I once was
> The girl in the mirror of your love

So what does this becoming look like? My current upheaval involves the mirror again. As I grow older, facing the loss of face is frightening. Like aging sidewalks, my skin must also submit to the unrelenting forces of nature. I've gotten a certain amount of attention for my looks over the years, and though I am loathe to admit it, I know I've built some of my identity around this skin-deep person. How much? I'm finding out. I have no choice. There's no going back.

Today I am the woman in the morning mirror, the one my family and friends see more than I do. But I also exist in my thoughts, my prayers, my past, and my future.

It takes a lot of effort just to *be* in the moment. Just to be. As I write these words, I can count down the months to forty. Significant, yet meaning less and less to me as The Day approaches. I am wrestling, however, with the persistent reminders in my body and on my face. I'm repeating refrains I've mostly heard in third person. This age must be the birthplace of the saying, "Youth is wasted on the young."

❋

Am I still becoming? What am I becoming? I am a follower of Jesus. I love Him. He first loved me. What's the basis of that love? His choice, not my loveliness. Yet He created me, so I must be beautiful in some way. He certainly will finish what He's begun. I want to know more and more about this.

Recently, as I was getting ready for a party, I became aware of two trains of thought alternating in my head. First, I thought of who would be there at my friend's home and how I would want them to perceive me. Of course, my goal would be to make a good outward impression. I guess I just wanted admiration. So I chose my clothes and applied my makeup accordingly.

Meanwhile, the second train of thought went in quite a different direction. I thought about the other invitees and what they might need. Would someone be as nervous as I was and find encouragement in a warm smile and conversation? Could I give someone at the party a glimpse of a chink in my armor and thus dispel any impressions that I have it all together? Maybe even let my looks be less than perfect? That would mean caring more about preparing my heart than my face. Could I really go there ready to give something lasting rather than leave something fleeting?

As author Constance Rhodes points out, living to inspire is more fulfilling than living to impress. I still need to get that truth past my head and into my heart. I'd better start practicing.

Have you ever known a beautiful woman you forgot was beautiful simply because you couldn't stand who she was on the inside? I mean, at some point you saw her as a pretty face, but getting to know her meant forgetting about the outside. In the same way, I've known some not-really-great-looking people who are so attractive to me. Their beauty is not about their looks at all, but about their inward radiance and open countenance. That's how I want to be.

I want to be a welcoming woman with whom people feel at ease, able to share their weaknesses. Just as the people I love and want to be with most have usually moved way beyond my visual awareness of them, I want to move beyond my awareness of the visual impression I might be making. I want to attract people with my lack of needing their approval at all. How can I become more becoming?

I think aging is a huge part of the sanctification process. Before I say more, though, I want to wonder a bit at our obsession with youth. Is it completely off-base? I've often imagined what Adam and Eve might have looked like. Were they comparable to humans in their early twenties, with strong bodies and clear, seamless skin?

There's a reason youth is beautiful to us. I think wrinkles arrived with the snake. I think disease and decay set in when the first couple sold out. Death is the payment due us for our sin; a natural process only as a result of the Fall. I believe the beauty of youth is God's everlasting design for us. Only it won't be called *youth* in heaven, because that word denotes the existence of time, and we know there will be no time in heaven. We'll all just be great looking inside and out in eternity!

⚹

Now about sanctification. Living in God's direct gaze is excruciating and invigorating. He's got designs on my heart and won't take no for an answer. He'll never leave well enough alone. He'll even send upheavals to keep me coming back to Him. He'll allow the ache and sag of life and time to peel away layers of the made-up me, even if it gets ugly. I have moments of clarity when I see myself—for a split second—in the perfect mirror of His love. In these moments of sanity, I realize I have nothing to lose; it's already all gone. The real me emerges, and I have nothing to hide.

In 2 Corinthians 3:18, Paul talked about how the beauty of Christ's gospel is so much better than the fading glory of the old covenant. He wrote, "But we all, with unveiled face, beholding as in a mirror the glory of the Lord" (NKJV). This means we reflect His glory in our own lives, and thus our glory is ever increasing. But we hold this treasure in common containers so that only God gets the glory. "Therefore we do not lose heart. Even though our outward man is perishing, yet the inward man is being renewed day by day" (2 Corinthians 4:16, NKJV).

So Paul tells us not to focus on what we see, because these things are temporary. Rather, we should dwell on what is unseen, because these things are eternal. Sounds like words of life to me. Outwardly I am wasting away, but inside I'm becoming quite lovely!

We were born to be glorious. Remember, He set eternity in our hearts. He calls us His children, friends, and lovers, meant for intimacy. He set His sights on you and me before the foundation of the world. "I am my lover's and my lover is mine," said Solomon.[2] That's a pretty strong basis for relationship.

This security in relationship allows me to blossom, take risks, and be brave. I am secure in Christ. From this foundation I am free to branch out, to bloom in new ways, and to brush against other people's windows. I can quit worrying about how I look and start seeing inside the lives of others that are unfolding around me. Here is where my reflecting must begin and continue. When my daughters and my friends sense this freedom in me, they will be inspired to move that way too. We'll dance before the mirror and know that we are lovely, spinning in the glorious freedom of the children of God. Then we can all sing the refrain together:

I am becoming
Your love becomes me

Therefore we do not lose heart. Though outwardly we are wasting away, yet inwardly we are being renewed day by day.

—THE APOSTLE PAUL (2 Corinthians 4:16, NIV)

Giving What Has Been Given

Been Given

Phil Keaggy

A s I look back over the many twists and turns of my life, I can't help but recognize that none of us can really advance to a place of being without the loving influence and impact of others in our lives. For me, much of that influence has come from my family.

I was born the ninth of ten children to James and Marguerite Keaggy on March 23, 1951. We lived on a farm in Youngstown, Ohio. It was not a commercial farm, but a humble number of acres with a little house that still stands.

As a toddler I shared a bedroom with five older brothers (the eldest, Jim, was killed in a car accident when I was just two). Our sister Peg, who had married before I was born, lived with her husband in a small apartment above the garage next to our house. Another sister, Mary Ellen, who is twenty years older than I, was a beautiful singer and actress who had moved off to Hollywood.

Rounding out the family was my baby sister, Geri Beth, who very much resembles our dear mom and to this day is especially close to me. With so many family members making up the walls of my young world, I felt welcome, secure, and loved.

Dad, a World War II navy veteran, was a structural ironworker who worked as hard as any man could to provide a humble income for our family. He was also all about providing fun and adventure. When I was just four years old, Dad made a quarter-mile racetrack for our motorcycles and Midget racecars. He then worked with my brothers to create a hill-climb course that soon drew a lot of interest from local bikers. I can still remember Sunday afternoon picnics and watching races at the track. Our home movies of these events show me running up the hill with our dogs while the riders were taking a break. Sometimes I'd even be on my little bicycle with its training wheels, buzzing down the quarter-mile track in between races, having a grand time!

And Mom… There was no one like her in the whole world, to me—to all of us. She was the most gracious and loving person I've ever known. You felt welcomed if you were a guest in our house, and she made each of us children feel we were the most special child alive. Even today when I speak to my brothers and sisters about Mom, one would get the impression that each of us had a special connection to her loving heart. I'll never forget her love, patience, and kindness.

✗

There was always music in the house where I grew up. Mary Ellen was a singer, and my brothers would bring home records of their favorite music, so I was introduced early on to an array of diverse talent. There was the classical music Dave loved, such as Mantovani and Ravel. Mike brought home recordings of great vocal groups and soloists. Bill, who is eleven years older than I, had Elvis in his collection. Fats Domino, the Ink Spots, Johnnie Ray, the Everly Brothers, the Hilltoppers, and others were playing on Dave's Magnavox turntable all the time, and I loved them all.

But it was Scotty Moore, Elvis's guitar player, who really caught my ear. I was entranced by his guitar sound when I heard Elvis's 1956 recording of "My Baby Left Me," and from that day on, I began collecting Elvis's music.

In those days my world was music, records, record players, and speakers of all shapes and sizes. It was a wonder to me how music could be recorded and played through a needle, a tone arm, tubes, an amplifier, wires, and speakers—all to my delight! Every now and then a particular song would catch my ear and grab my heart, each magical tune foundational to my becoming a musician. And no one in my family ever discouraged this influence.

In 1956 the music briefly came to a halt when I had an accident that resulted in my losing the middle finger on my right hand. I had gone to get a drink of water at the old water pump behind our house, and when I stood on its old wooden base, the foundation gave way. Suddenly the pump broke through the base, catching my hand between the faucet and the concrete.

As I screamed in pain and terror, I saw my father racing down the hill from our house to rescue me. I had never before or since seen my father run so fast. He took me up in his arms and called Mary Ellen, who drove us to the hospital. I was frightened, but I vividly recall how my dad, wearing his red-and-black plaid shirt, held me to his chest and comforted me. My mother soon joined us at the hospital and suffered there with her little boy.

I remember the ether and falling into unconsciousness. Brown paper bags full of little toys greeted me when I awoke, but it was the visits of dear family members that soothed the anguish of this traumatized little boy.

Just two weeks after my accident, while I was still in bandages, my little sister, Geri Beth, lost her big toe in a bicycle accident. With so many children in our family, it seemed inevitable that accidents would happen, but it was a somber time at the Keaggy's. Mom and Dad were feeling a lot of pain, remembering also the loss of our eldest brother, Jim, whose accident had occurred just a few years earlier.

Through these and other trials, my mom never lost her faith in God. She was a praying, godly woman. And how blessed we were to know her comfort! She was always there for us kids as well as for Dad who worked so hard and suffered from harsh memories of the war. Even though Mom had a lot of demands on her, I can't recall a moment when she displayed an unloving attitude. Through her faithful example, the influence of a loving God was ever present in our home.

I believe that I am a Christian today because of the prayers of a mother who believed in a loving God and who prayed that someday He would use me to inspire and bring hope to others through the talent He has blessed me with.

I recall the remarkable sense of discovering my "being" a few years later. I was ten at the time, the same year I received my first real guitar—a Sears Silvertone acoustic. I distinctly remember examining my hands one day while visiting Gram, my mom's mother, and being overwhelmed with realizing my "aliveness." I felt a sense of wonder and a bit of trembling as well. I was growing up and, in a child's way, realizing that I had a purpose that was bigger than I was, though I wouldn't fully understand it until nine years later.

In the meantime I endured school like every kid, though I was never studious. (Mom said I had brains but just didn't apply myself.) I was insecure because of my short stature and self-conscious about my missing finger. I remember I would raise only my left hand when asking questions. In third grade I had my First Communion photo taken with my class, and while all the kids were proudly smiling at the camera, there I was examining my missing finger. I wish I still had that photo—I was totally in my own world that day, and that's how I felt much of the time.

On Christmas Day 1962, my brother Dave surprised me with my first electric guitar. I'll never forget that morning! Within a year I had learned some Beach Boys and other surf music, as well as some of Dick Dale's guitar work. I still had much to learn about jazz and classical players, but whenever I played, people would tell me I had a special gift. Dad was proud of me and would often ask me to play that "Strobee." He loved, as he called it, my "fast and fancy guitar playing." Soon after that, when I was in sixth grade, I heard the Beatles for the first time at my grandmother's home and felt another confirmation that music would be my life. At the time I had no idea of the impact these lads from Liverpool would have on the music culture that would follow in the wake of their success. All I knew was that something about the way their vocal blend fused with the tone of the electric guitars sent me running full of inspiration to my own guitar.

Looking back I can see that God used those early influences to shape and mold me to desire the world of music and art so that one day I could bring the message of the good news of His Son to others. At the time I had not yet accepted Christ as my Savior. But that day would soon come, spurred on by a tragedy I never expected.

✗

When I embraced the guitar as a child, I felt like a rocket that had been launched. Now I can see that through the challenges, trials, and temptations of the teenage years that followed, I was being prepared to give this gift back to my Creator-Redeemer, though I didn't know it yet.

On February 14, 1970, while I was on tour with my band, Glass Harp, my mom was the victim of a head-on collision. When she passed away several days later, I was devastated. It was during this time of grieving that I came to a point of decision. Through the loving encouragement of my sister Mary Ellen, I gave my heart, life, and music to Jesus. Of course the bigger truth of it all, as I've come to discover, is that He gave His heart for me. What a wonderful God and Friend!

In spite of the tragic loss of my mother, 1970 ended up being a year full of joy and freedom in many ways. It also presented new challenges, the first of which was to learn how to serve God with my music. From my place in the band, I began to openly share my newfound faith with the only audience I had: our fans. I felt a passion to do this. The Bible had become real to me. I had good news to sing and talk about, and I found myself sharing Christ both on and off the stage.

After recording four albums with Glass Harp, each of which stated my personal faith in Jesus, I felt led to leave the band. This was not an easy decision—we were very close as bandmates and friends. I had known two of my bandmates since childhood. Together we had shared the grand and exciting experience of becoming Decca recording artists and had worked hard to achieve local and limited national success. Still, I felt a pull to go out on my own, not knowing where it would take me.

In January 1971, a year before leaving the band, I met a young woman named Bernadette, who would become my wife. We married in July 1973, and for the past thirty years now, she has been my dearest and most beloved friend this side of heaven.

About six months before Bernadette and I got married, I recorded a collection of songs titled *What a Day*. No longer part of Glass Harp, I had no record label for this project until a man named Scott Ross heard it and believed it could be the debut album for a new label called New Song Records. In 1974 the album was released with limited distribution. As people came to listen to it, I received letters expressing the blessing of this little project. Within a couple of years, Word Records redistributed this album along with a second solo recording.

The earlier Glass Harp albums, combined with these solo efforts, opened doors for me to share in the music ministries of truly gifted artists such as Love Song, Paul Clark, Randy Stonehill, Barry McGuire, Honeytree, and others who were pioneers in the Christian music movement. Many albums came about in the years that followed, each representing my faith and my experiences walking with the Lord.

It was during this time that I went through some of the most difficult experiences of my life. Between 1975 and 1977, Bernadette and I suffered the loss of our babies—three premature boys in 1975, a son we named Ryan who lived only three days in 1976, and a four-month-old child in 1977.

Since those days, God has blessed Bernadette and me with three beautiful, healthy children—Alicia, Olivia, and Ian. These children, now mostly grown, are our truest treasures on this earth. But those earlier losses affected us deeply. While many songs were borne out of this painful season, at the end of it, I was dry. I longed for a way to express deeper feelings—feelings words couldn't describe.

This culminated in the 1978 recording of my first instrumental project, *The Master and the Musician*. This was a musical departure for me, and it satisfied a desire to play my heartstrings in a different way. Once again God was providing a new way for me to communicate His message to others through music.

✝

Many years of life lessons, frequent travel, and numerous recordings have only reinforced my desire to be the musician God wants me to be. I continually search for my voice artistically and seek new ways of expressing it. With a catalog of more than forty-five albums now, I still find much pleasure in the creative process. It's all a great adventure, one that might never have happened if not for the love and support of friends and family who have shaped and encouraged my development as an artist, a musician unto the Lord.

So in closing, I must say that I believe the art of being has to do with the art of giving, the art of loving, and with being in love. After all, Scripture tells us that "it is more blessed to give than to receive" (Acts 20:35, NIV), and that the only thing that really matters is "faith working through love" (Galatians 5:6, NASB). To believe we are important for who we are is to believe we have potential to love and give.

Music and the love of my family were gifts to me before I could do something to earn them or even realize how valuable they were. They are still gifts to me from above, and they continue to help me discover who I am.

As an artist I find no greater satisfaction than knowing that my gift of art holds significance and importance to another person. Each of us is fulfilled when we give out of who we are and find that our gift is received. As we continue to give of that which was given to us, we see a continual confirmation of our being. And that's why I carry on.

Give away your life; you'll find life given back, but not merely given back—given back with bonus and blessing.

—JESUS (Luke 6:38)

Lessons Learned Along

the Way

Constance **Rhodes** Interviews Gloria
Gaither and Her Best Friends, Joy
Mac**Kenzie** and Peggy Benson

When I called Gloria Gaither to ask if she would contribute her perspective to this book, I discovered that she had been talking about the theme of "being" for decades before my inquiry. Apparently my idea was nothing new to this woman who had written hundreds of songs now considered standards in our faith, and who had traveled the world for more days than I had even been alive. As a woman who has been in the public eye her entire adult life, Gloria had something none of the others on my list of artists could claim—more than forty years of seasoned experience in trying to balance her personal and professional lives.

A few months after our phone conversation, we met for breakfast and were joined by two of Gloria's closest friends, Joy MacKenzie and Peggy Benson. For the next hour and a half, I had the privilege of listening to these three women—each distinguished and accomplished in her own right—reminisce about their years of public life and the demands that go along with it, their respective life choices, and best of all, their friendship.

The following excerpt contains the intimate details of our discussion, and while the format is a little different from the other writings in this book, the truths Gloria and her friends shared are timeless and universal. I hope you enjoy them.

*

Constance: The first thing I'd like to ask you is how you've been able to find your identity in who you are instead of what you do. I imagine people always want something from you. How do you figure out who you are—the onstage Gloria and the personal Gloria—and somehow find that delicate balance between business, home life, friends, yourself, and God?

Gloria: Well, it's important to know that the minute you start believing your own press releases, you're in serious trouble. If your stage life becomes your life, then you have signed your own death certificate—emotionally, physically, spiritually, and eventually, publicly. And once that happens, there is nothing left but a shell.

Of course, the public helps create that shell, because if you've done anything that is significant or that people view as significant, you are placed on a pedestal. But what we seem to forget is that so often our success has little to do with us. Sometimes it simply happens—the timing of when we came along and did what we did somehow worked, but really, it's all a hoot. I mean, our whole life as the Gaithers could seem to be an accident—just a series of accidents. You know, we were just there in the right place at the right time. But God engineered it...

You know there's a wonderful book called *When God Winks*, which basically says that all of those accidents that seem to just happen are really God moving us into a certain place. There's also a great movie called *Sliding Doors*, which brings up a really interesting question: If choices and accidents in life happened in a different way, would we still eventually move to the same place? After all, maybe it doesn't have to be these sets of circumstances that are required for us to end up where we're supposed to be.

I think we take ourselves way too seriously sometimes. But I do think there are some key things that help when it comes to living in peace with who you are and with balancing your professional and personal lives. For me, finding peace in my personal life is easy, but my professional life can drive me nuts, which is why I've learned I can't take it too seriously. For example, publishers often require writers and artists to attend sales and/or radio conventions. While it is an ego trip to be invited, this is not the real world. Usually we are not succeeding as much as it may seem when we are accepted, flattered, and applauded, nor are we failing as much as we feel we are if we are ignored when some "newer, better" artist walks by. What I'm saying is that the real world is who I am when I'm alone in an elevator. The real world is what happens in our house on the hill in Alexandria, Indiana. The real world is responding to someone with a lost kid or a broken heart. So if we take success too seriously, we're setting ourselves up to fail.

Going further, in making peace with who you are, it's also important to decide where to live. You have to live someplace, but I would advise against living in your professional place. Give yourself enough distance to keep perspective. I know it may sound crazy, but Bill and I chose not to live in Nashville. We live in the same small town where Bill was born, and our rationale has been that if we can't do it in Alexandria, Indiana, then we can't do it anywhere.

After all, it doesn't matter so much what the music industry thinks. What matters is what the people think—you know, the people at the truck stop and the bakery and the bank, and the people you went to high school with, and the people who are living regular lives. What do they think? Does it work? You've got to stay where you can be real.

Joy: Where you can breathe.

Gloria: Yes, and for us that means our small town in Indiana. For others it might mean just finding your own space or church family or circle of friends.

The next thing we had to do was establish priorities. From the beginning Bill and I said, "Okay, here are our priorities: We've got to serve the Lord, we've got to love each other, we've got to raise our kids, and if there's anything left, we'll do some concerts." We haven't always kept that balance, but it's our goal.

And even in our professional lives, we had to set priorities. For example, since we can't be everywhere at the same time, we decided early on that, for us, writing would be more important than traveling and performing. We feel that if we can create something that will outlive us, which other people can use and adapt to their situations, then that is more important to us than doing a certain thing the way we do it for a certain crowd or setting or time.

Jesus was a wonderful model when He said, "I need to go away. If I stay here, then I am the locale of your strength. If I go away, I will send you the Holy Spirit, who will teach you all things…and trust Me, that's a better deal." The Holy Spirit is portable. He is with us always and everywhere.

But even our writing has had to take a backseat to the priorities of our personal life. Family is primary. The good thing about kids and family is that they don't let you get away with being fake. In anyone's professional life there are times when illusions are created through imaging, marketing, positioning, and politicking. Sometimes we need a three-year-old who tells it like it is.

I also make it a priority to be involved in even the most mundane life chores. I think it helps to take out the garbage, shovel the walk, clean the commode, fold your own towels, and mow your own lawn. Timewise, I know I can't do it all, but even when I have help, I don't want to lose touch with these daily things. As simple as they might seem, they are all very important parts of life, and they have everything to do with reality.

A third key is to find good long-term friends who knew you

before it [success] all happened and will still be there when it's over. And in the meantime, they know you are not the "imaged" person everyone else sees. You don't have the all-together marriage, you're not the perfect parent. And you're not the glamorous, skinny person people see on stage or on TV.

Peggy: Yeah, you should see Gloria when she has her pantyhose off!

Gloria: *(laughing)* Nobody deserves to see that!

Peggy: Here's an example of what Gloria's talking about. Three years ago one of my boys was killed. He fell 150 feet. You can imagine the shock I was in, and since my husband had died a few years earlier, I felt alone in my grief. During this difficult time, I don't know where Gloria was, but whatever she was doing, she dropped it and came to me.

Later, when a friend heard that Gloria had come, she asked, "What did Gloria do?" I think my friend expected that Gloria would have dropped to her knees and started praying, because she has often been called on to do that in her ministry. As I stopped to consider this, I suddenly remembered just what Gloria had done. It was something that really endeared her to me.

You know, she's always trying to get me to eat better, and she knows what I like to eat. So she made me go sit down on the couch, and she went into the kitchen, peeled an apple, and cut it in little tiny slivers the way I like it. That's true friendship. To me she wasn't "Gloria the Celebrity;" she was my friend. Over the years we've shared a special bond—Joy, Gloria, and me, and it's been an incredible thing. *(nods around the table)*

Gloria: The fourth thing we must remember is that any kind of professional life is going to be short. In our line of business, it is especially short—if we last five years in the limelight it's a long career. Through some miracle we've been at this for forty years now, which is probably some kind of record. But even though we've managed to survive for so long, we still know it's transient.

Bill and I often tell young artists, "Don't make your high year your watermark." This is an important principle because for a lot of people who find success, the sudden change in income can greatly affect them in a way that can be negative. One minute they're starving, and the next minute they're buying fancy cars like they think this is the new norm.

As success comes, we can't allow ourselves to get to the point where what Bill would call our "monthly nut" dictates our life and/or our ministry. If we were to set our lifestyle at the high watermark, we would have higher house payments and car payments and all this stuff to pay for. And so this image we think we have to have starts dictating our lifestyle, which in turn starts dictating our ministry, instead of the other way around. This is a dangerous place to be, and it will prevent us from effectively following the call God has on our lives.

Joy: In addition to the things Gloria has said, for people who have multiple lives going on—a professional life, a home life, a business life, and extended friendships—I think we sometimes get hung up trying to achieve perfection in all of these places.

What it finally boils down to is this: How are you going to spend today? Somewhere along the way I came to the realization that I cannot be a great mother and a great teacher and a great writer and a great wife and a great friend and a great daughter-in-law and all the fifty other roles I play in my life. But then I realized that I could be good at all of these things, but not on the same day.

Of course, it's not like you get up in the morning and say, "Today I'm going to be a good mother, and tomorrow I'm going to be a good teacher," (or writer, or whatever those other roles might be). But we must accept the fact that we can't be all of these things at the same time.

We only need to get to the point where we are satisfied at the end of the day, thankful that we were able to do something good as a mother, or as a teacher, or whatever our role is. You can't always make conscious decisions about this, but you can ask the Lord to help map that out for you.

I learned to begin days saying, "Okay, Lord, here we go again. It's Your day, and You've got to show me where the paths are, because otherwise I'm going to dive into something, and I'm going to spend my whole day writing and making everybody else just miserable."

Then you're so short of days that you cut yourself out of everything, in terms of nourishing yourself, and you feel guilty if you take time to get your nails done, or if you plan to meet a friend for lunch, and you don't come back until four o'clock. I remember one day I went to lunch with a friend, and we forgot to pick up our kids from school! You can get so frustrated and so overwrought that you get to thinking you're not good at anything.

Peggy: (smiling) Well, it probably is hard for you; you spread yourself too thin.

Joy: Well, you have to take care of yourself, not in the selfish kind of philosophy that says, "I am wonderful, I am me, everything is about me." But we must learn to take moments to actually close the bathroom door and take time to breathe.

With that, Gloria's cell phone rang. As she turned to answer it, I checked my watch and realized our meeting had gone thirty minutes over our originally scheduled time. As much as I would have liked to chat with these ladies all morning, I knew our time together was quickly coming to an end. But I also knew I had gotten what I came for.

As we walked out into the sun-filled lobby, we all exchanged hugs before heading our separate ways, and even though I knew I may never see these three women again, I felt the warmth of their friendship extending even to me.

In a lot of ways, that was the biggest lesson I learned that day:

the priceless value of just being with friends—talking, remembering, laughing. Simple exchanges of chatter that left us richer because we had shared these moments with one another.

> Be still, and know that I am God...
> Be still, and know...
> Be still...
> Be...
>
> —GOD (Psalm 46:10, KJV)

Notes

Little Snail

1. John Ortberg, *Love Beyond Reason* (Grand Rapids: Zondervan, 1998), 103.

2. Ortberg, *Love Beyond Reason*, 104.

The Myth of Clarity

1. John Kavanaugh, *America* 173, no. 3 (29 July 1995): 38. Quoted in Brennan Manning, *Ruthless Trust* (San Francisco: HarperSanFrancisco, 2002), 5.

Be the Story

1. T-Bone Burnett, interview by JesusJournal.com, February 23, 2002. Found at www.jesusjournal.com/jj_culture/music/ music_burnett.html.

It's Not About Me

1. Tammy Trent, "Rescue Me," © 2003 Pete Orta and Tammy Trent/Mexican Gunfighter Music (administered by ION Music Administration)/ASCAP/tammy b music/BMI. All rights reserved. Used by permission.

Sixty-Five Miles an Hour

1. C. S. Lewis, *The Weight of Glory and Other Addresses* (New York: Macmillan, 1965), 18-19.

The Value of Wasting Time

1. Antoine de Saint Exupéry, *The Little Prince*, trans. Katherine Woods (New York: Harcourt, Brace & World, 1943), 87-88.

Becoming—The Girl in the Mirror

1. Christine Dente, "Becoming," © 2002 Christine Dente/Mighty Grey Music/Lil Yella House Music/Dayspring Music, LLC/BMI. All rights reserved. Used by permission.

2. Author's paraphrase of Song of Songs 2:16.

About the Contributors

When I set out to compile this book, I had several possible contributors in mind, many of whom I had worked with personally while in the music business. As the project developed, however, I felt God was continually reminding me to remain flexible and to trust that He would shape the book as He saw fit. In the end there was no denying that He had indeed brought together an incredibly diverse group of voices. I am honored to have had so many creative and thoughtful artists join me in this endeavor, and I wish to share with you some of what makes each of them so special.

Sara Groves

I first heard Sara's name in 1999 while at a music-industry business dinner. Prompted by the inevitable question, "What's in your CD player?" one of the guests began raving about an unsigned artist named Sara Groves. At that time her name was new to most of us, but it wasn't long before she left an indelible mark on Christian music. In her no-frills, down-to-earth way, Sara sings about the realities of life with a vulnerability and honesty that is disarming. I was already a fan when I heard her 2002 release *All Right Here* and knew that I had to ask her to join this project.

Listening to the song "Every Minute," I was stunned to hear Sara sing the line *"It's the fine art of being who I am…"* At the time I knew she had a lot on her plate, so I hesitated to ask her to participate. But when I heard that line, I knew I had to at least try. I'm glad I did.

To learn more about Sara, visit www.saragroves.com.

Gabriel Wilson (Rock 'n' Roll Worship Circus)

I love the theme that Gabriel chose for his chapter because—to be honest—I, too, was guilty of judging him the first time I saw him. It was Gospel Music Association Week 2002, and as I walked into the jam-packed lobby of the Nashville Convention Center, I couldn't help but notice this band with wild hair, strange jewelry, and outlandish clothing. *Here we go again!* I remember thinking. *Someone else who's trying to prove something.* But that night my preconceived notions were shattered as I experienced one of the most musically brilliant and spiritually passionate concerts I had ever attended. There was no denying the fresh new work that God was doing through this band, and I was humbled by the flippant judgment I had levied just a few hours earlier. Indeed, we are all different, and it is whose we are that makes us one. Thank you, Gabe, for reminding us of that fact.

To learn more about Gabriel and his band, Rock 'n' Roll Worship Circus, visit www.worshipcircus.com.

Ginny Owens

We met over Mexican food in Franklin, Tennessee. As I shared with Ginny my vision for this book, I found myself slightly unnerved by the fact that she could not see me. Suddenly aware of my overwhelming dependence on visual cues, I began to worry about how I was coming across. Confronted by my own insecurities, I had to laugh a little; here we were, talking about just being who we are, and all I could think about was how I was being perceived! Since that time, what I have come to learn most about Ginny is that she has never allowed her blindness to define who she is. In fact, many of her fans don't even know she is blind until they meet her in person. Indeed, as is true for most of us, Ginny's greatest challenge is not what she *can't* see, but rather in finding the courage to be obedient to what she *can* see: God's daily instruction for her life. May we all be so bold.

To learn more about Ginny visit www.ginnyowens.com.

Paul Meany (Mute Math)

I'll never forget the first time I heard Paul's former band, Earthsuit. I was at a staff retreat with the record company I used to work for, and the president of our label previewed for us some new artists who had recently been signed. From the first note of the first song, I knew these guys were special. They broke every mold—lyrically, musically, and stylistically, and all I could think about was how to worm my way into working on their upcoming release. Unfortunately, as Paul indicates in his chapter, Earthsuit's incredible uniqueness proved to be both their greatest strength and their ultimate undoing, as it was tough to market a band that stood so far to the left of traditional lines. But while their album may not have been a commercial success, it was a watershed to many of us who needed a fresh blast of creativity and inspiration. As Paul moves ahead into new musical territories, I look forward to being challenged again to consider that life is not always black-and-white—there's a lot happening in the gray.

To learn more about Paul, Earthsuit, and Paul's new band Mute Math, visit www.mutemath.com.

Jill Phillips

It was my husband AJ who first introduced me to the incredible talent of Jill Phillips. In 2001 AJ was significantly impacted by one of her songs, and several months later her independent release *God and Money* was still the primary spin on his stereo. AJ seemed unable to describe exactly how her music had affected him, but I knew it had come along at a very important point in his own personal spiritual journey, and for that I was grateful. Jill's music is not about Jill. She definitely pulls from her own experiences in creating her art, but the overarching themes are God's grace, His provision, and the working of His ultimate purpose for each one of us. Jill's own life is a testament to these things. While she has faced her share of disappointments, challenges, and sorrows along life's road, she still finds joy and comfort in exploring God's promises and in sharing that journey with the rest of us.

To learn more about Jill, visit www.jillphillips.com.

Matthew Odmark (Jars of Clay)

"I have become convinced that it is God's desire for us to live courageously and thankfully in the gift of each moment," wrote Matt to the Jars of Clay fan list in 1995. Nearly ten years later, he continues to live out this principle. Even so, as we discussed possible themes for his chapter, I don't think either of us imagined what a hard hitting challenge Matt would end up bringing forth. When talking about the so-called art of being, it can be easy to think only of one part of the equation: relaxing…breathing…taking time off from the grind of life. As Matt so eloquently points out, however, truly being who God created us to be also requires courageously embracing a story that is bigger than we are—a story we might not choose for ourselves. But there is comfort in knowing that the Author of our story is the One who sees the end from the beginning. We must only believe…

To learn more about Matt and Jars of Clay, visit www.jarsofclay.com.

Tammy Trent

The first time I met Tammy, her husband Trent was with her. In fact, they were rarely apart. They were like two lovebirds who had never heard the phrase "the honeymoon's over." And with good reason! As overly glowing as Tammy's description of Trent may seem, I knew him well enough to know that every word she's written is true. His death was a shock not only to Tammy and the rest of his family but to so many of us who couldn't imagine how she was going to function now that her best friend and soul mate was gone. Less than a year later, I gingerly asked Tammy whether she might consider contributing to this project. It seemed almost insensitive to ask, but I felt strongly that I was supposed to. Still reeling from the pain of her loss, Tammy nonetheless graciously nodded her consent. "There are just some things that you know are right," she said, "and for me, this is one of those things."

To learn more about Tammy, visit www.tammytrent.com.

Jonathan Foreman (Switchfoot)

While I have been inspired and challenged by every artist involved in this project, Jon's participation holds special meaning. Throughout his relatively young career as lead writer, visionary, and vocalist for the band Switchfoot, Jon has been touching on themes way beyond his years. Things like the fact that this life is quickly passing by and that in God's economy, it's not what any of us has that matters. For most of us, it takes hitting thirty to begin to grasp these truths; Jon's been writing about them since he was in his late teens. It was while I was working on the marketing for Switchfoot's third release, *Learning to Breathe,* that their music had its greatest impact on my life. A powerful lyric in the song "Dare You to Move" became the final catalyst in my own journey from doing to being. When it came time to invite artists to join this effort, I knew this book would feel incomplete without Jon's involvement. Thankfully, he agreed to sign on.

To learn more about Jonathan and his band, Switchfoot, visit www.switchfoot.com.

Ashley Cleveland

"She sings like she means it. She writes like she means it. I think she means it," John Hiatt has said of Ashley, who toured as part of his band in the late eighties. Indeed, if there's one thing you can count on from this two-time Grammy-winning, rock 'n' roll renegade, it's that she says what she means, and she means what she says. Knowing she was never one to hide her true colors, I anticipated that Ashley would contribute something special to this project, but I had no idea just how powerful her story would be. As I read her first draft, I was pierced by the honest portrayal of one who has seen some of the harshest realities of life and somehow found the strength to lift a hand to God for help. Whether or not we choose to admit it, there are reflections of Ashley's story in all of us—a gentle reminder that only through dying to that which we hold so dear can we truly experience the life God has for us.

To learn more about Ashley, visit www.ashleycleveland.com.

Don and Lori Chaffer (Waterdeep)

In 1998 I traveled with some coworkers to the headquarters of a large Christian bookstore chain in Oklahoma. It was a "learning" trip, and over lunch we grilled the music manager on which artists were selling best in his stores. Since our company represented many of the top-selling artists in the industry, we were surprised to hear him rave about a group we had never heard of. Over the next few years, however, we came to appreciate the grass-roots phenomenon that is Waterdeep, the band headed by Don and Lori Chaffer. Coloring entirely outside traditional CCM lines, Waterdeep has made an art of infusing relationship and community into everything they do. Their philosophy is simple, yet profound: "We want to be part of a community that leads our generation into a deeper relationship with God," says Don. "With that support as our platform, we want to speak eternal Truth into a culture that has seen the dissolution of truth." Bravo!

To learn more about Don and Lori and their band, Waterdeep, visit www.waterdeep.com.

Linford Detweiler (Over the Rhine)

After resigning my job in August of 2000, the first thing I did in my own journey to "be" was to take a road trip. Packed up in my Honda, I drove nine hours to my childhood home of Brighton, Michigan, and then another five hours north to Drummond Island, where my father has a cabin on the water. On the trip I had plenty of time to reflect, time made more meaningful by the hauntingly beautiful recording *Good Dog, Bad Dog* by Over the Rhine. In this age of manufactured pop music, Over the Rhine's Linford Detweiler and Karin Bergquist have somehow resisted the trappings of commercial success, choosing instead to continue creating art that allows time and space to breathe—a precious commodity on the journey toward being. When it came time to pull this book together, a friend connected me with Linford, and just as I had hoped, the result was as beautiful as the music I have come to love so much.

To learn more about Linford and his band, Over the Rhine, visit www.overtherhine.com.

Christine Dente (Out of the Grey)

The first time I heard Christine's voice was 1992. I'd been given a sampler of new artists, and on it was the song "Wishes" by Out of the Grey, the duo comprised of Christine Dente and her husband, Scott. I was an instant fan! Never before had I heard someone sing in such a creative and unusual way. And she was beautiful too— you could see that from the photo on the cover. Several years later I was working for Out of the Grey's label and had the opportunity to observe Christine a little more closely. As she describes in her chapter, she was often quiet and distant, as if she didn't know just how wonderful and beautiful and talented she truly was. What I now understand is that she, like so many of us, was on the road of discovering who she was beyond her talents or her reflection in the mirror. I am so grateful for her vulnerability on this subject, as it is one that hits very close to home.

To learn more about Christine Dente, visit www.christinedente.com.

Phil Keaggy

In 1988 one of my favorite songs was Phil Keaggy's hit "Sunday's Child." Never did I imagine I would one day meet this legendary guitarist face to face! Seven years later I picked Phil up at the Montreal Airport to bring him to an industry event hosted by the label I was working for. As we headed to the venue, I made a wrong turn and proceeded to get us quite lost. We were pressed for time, and Phil could have gotten quite frustrated with me, yet he remained calm, quietly offering kind words along the way. We eventually found the venue, and the evening was a great success. Afterward, as the guests applauded Phil's extraordinary talent, all I could think about was his meek and giving nature. Now that I've had the opportunity to hear more of his story, I have an even better appreciation for what is undoubtedly his greatest success: recognizing the eternal importance of giving our lives away.

To learn more about Phil Keaggy, visit www.philkeaggy.com.

Gloria Gaither

I was first given a window into the multifaceted personality of Gloria Gaither while I was working with a small label headed by one of her longtime friends. Until that time I had known little of Gloria, other than the fact that she represented half of the wildly popular phenomenon that is "the Gaithers"—I had no idea just how brilliant, creative, and insightful she was in other areas. My first glimpse of her unique perspective was through a poem she had written titled "Poets," which she graciously allowed me to post on my Web site. Then I attended one of the Gaithers' annual, sold-out "Praise Gathering" events and got to see even more of what makes this lady so special. As a woman who has spent more than forty years balancing the demands of marriage, motherhood, and full-time ministry, Gloria has a perspective on life that has been shaped and tested by time itself. It is an honor to include her in this book.

To learn more about Gloria, the Gaithers, and their ministry, visit www.gaithernet.com.

To read more about *The Art of Being,* please visit www.artofbeingbook.com.

About the Compiler and Editor

Erick Anderson

CONSTANCE RHODES is the founder and director of FINDING*balance*.com, an organization dedicated to eating, image, and lifestyle-management issues. She is also the author of *Life Inside the "Thin" Cage: A Personal Look into the Hidden World of the Chronic Dieter* and frequently speaks on the topic of disordered eating and the importance of embracing our true selves. A former marketing director for Sparrow Records, a division of EMI Music, Constance was led to pursue this compilation by her appreciation for the work of contemporary musicians. She and her husband, AJ, live in Franklin, Tennessee, with their two sons.

www.FINDINGbalance™.com
eating   image   life

"I don't have an eating disorder. I just watch what I eat..."

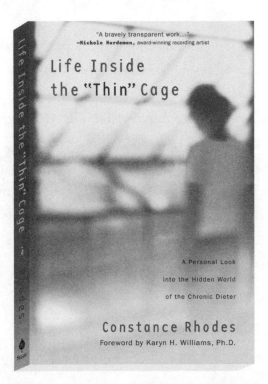

Yeah, right. It's perfectly normal to skip meals, fixate on calories, fat grams, and carbs, starve during the week, live at the gym, binge on the weekends, obsess about weight and what others think…sure, it's perfectly normal…or is it?

Life Inside the "Thin" Cage offers an insider's look into one of life's most private struggles and will change your perspective on the ever-elusive pursuit of 'thin.'

Available in bookstores everywhere.

SHAW BOOKS
www.shawbooks.com